'At last, an extremely readable sensible but deeply nuanced and well researched work in a field full of over-blown claims, scaremongering or complacency. This book will be of huge benefit and indeed, relief, to professionals, parents and indeed anyone interested in some of the most fundamental issues of our time'.

Dr Graham Music, *Consultant Child & Adolescent Psychotherapist at the Tavistock and Portman Clinics, London, UK*

'From the workings of the human brain, written in an easy-to-understand fashion, to trauma, gaming, social media, addiction and everything in-between. Cath takes us on a journey of her vast experience discussing the online world; the difficulties many of us face with children, the myths and realities and, most importantly, clear and practical guidance. This book is a timely breath of fresh air and a must-have for any professional that works with children or for parents who want to understand more about the online lives of their children'.

Alan Mackenzie, *Online Safety Specialist and Founding Member of AACOSS, UK*

'Human behaviour has developed over thousands of years of social evolution and interaction and yet, in a very short time, the advent of technology seems to have upended much of what we perceive as the accepted norm. Or has it? Cath Knibbs provides a pragmatic insight into how these new online technologies and experiences map against current psychological theory and encourages the reader to focus on what the real challenges may be, rather than what the latest media panic tells us. Are we addicted to technology? How can we identify vulnerability? Why does child online gaming trigger so much fear for parents? How might fake news impact on our ability to assess truth or morality? Not only are these considerations held up to the mirror of current psychological research but effective strategies are offered for adults to support and manage the children in their care. Written with a clear eye and accessible approach, this book is a wonderful read for any adult yearning to understand their child's fascination with online technologies'.

Ken Corish, *Online Safety Director, South West Grid for Learning, UK*

'In her new breakout book, Cath Knibbs presents an essential ethnographic exploration into the new cyber world our children are being raised in. What is cyber-psychology, cyber-trauma, & digital parenting? What is E-attachment and how might it impact your child's developing sense of sense, ability for self-regulation, and capacity to develop meaningful relationships? The cyber world is changing us all. The neuroscience-backed insights Cath Knibbs presents are a much needed lamp to guide parents, therapists, educators and, most importantly, children out of the matrix'.

Dr Brent T. Hogarth, *Clinical Sports Psychologist and Head Coach at the Flow Research Collective*

Children, Technology and Healthy Development

How can adults keep children safe and healthy online now and in the future? How can we thrive alongside technology? This highly accessible book unpacks the latest psychological research, attachment theory and neurobiology to offer parents and professionals insight into how technology impacts children's development and how to navigate our lives online.

Catherine Knibbs shares her extensive experience to reveal what we know about human behaviour in cyberspace, and particularly that of children using devices, consoles and social media platforms. She offers a deeper understanding of how and why children engage online and shows parents and professionals how, rather than being overwhelmed by the dangers and pathologies of cyberspace, we can learn to support children in using technology healthily. She covers key topics including social media use and abuse, the impact of screen time, issues around gaming and extreme behaviours online. By the end of this book, you will be able to understand your child better and have an understanding of what is happening in their minds, brains and bodies in relation to the technological and digital world.

Children, Technology and Healthy Development is for all parents and professionals in psychology, education, social care and the police who are concerned with understanding how we support children in an online world. It will also be valuable reading for those in tech design interested in the impact of technology on the developing human.

Catherine Knibbs is a Clinical and Academic Researcher; Consultant in the fields of Cybertrauma and Online Harms, Director for Privacy4 Ltd, and a United Kingdom Council for Psychotherapy–Accredited Child and Adult Trauma Psychotherapist.

Children, Technology and Healthy Development

How to Help Kids Be Safe and Thrive Online

Catherine Knibbs

Routledge
Taylor & Francis Group

LONDON AND NEW YORK

First published 2022
by Routledge
2 Park Square, Milton Park, Abingdon, Oxon OX14 4RN

and by Routledge
605 Third Avenue, New York, NY 10158

Routledge is an imprint of the Taylor & Francis Group, an informa business

British Library Cataloguing-in-Publication Data
A catalogue record for this book is available from the British Library

Library of Congress Cataloging-in-Publication Data
Names: Knibbs, Catherine, author.
Title: Children, technology and healthy development : how to help
  kids be safe and thrive online / Catherine Knibbs.
Description: First Edition. | New York : Routledge, 2022. |
  Includes bibliographical references and index.
Identifiers: LCCN 2021015763 (print) | LCCN 2021015764
  (ebook) | ISBN 9780367770112 (Hardback) | ISBN
  9780367770150 (Paperback) | ISBN 9781003169390 (eBook)
Subjects: LCSH: Internet and children. | Child development.
Classification: LCC HQ784.I58 K64 2022 (print) | LCC HQ784.I58
  (ebook) | DDC 004.67/8083—dc23
LC record available at https://lccn.loc.gov/2021015763
LC ebook record available at https://lccn.loc.gov/2021015764

ISBN: 9780367770112 (hbk)
ISBN: 9780367770150 (pbk)
ISBN: 9781003169390 (ebk)

DOI: 10.4324/9781003169390

Typeset in Bembo
by Apex CoVantage, LLC

To my children for keeping me grounded, to one of my faithful companions who sadly died as the book was completed and for keeping me moving throughout and to the life that led me here with all its ups and downs.

Contents

SECTION II
Gaming: pitfalls, positives and processes: how to help   81

SECTION III
Social media: relationships in the palm of your
hand: the what, why and how to help   129

Preface

Human beings are social creatures; we tend to live in groups, mate for life and rarely do well when ostracised from groups or choose to live like a hermit. Given the nature of the lockdown of 2020, this has become all too apparent in the management of our own mental health and that of the rest of the world. During this time, it has resulted in so many of us going online and spending time in this virtual '**cyberspace**' (where we nowadays have the tech and accessibility, of course). This book has been written for you from my 30-plus years of using, working with and being fascinated by technology, so you can understand how human development in the ever-growing presence of technology is influenced and may be changing us and our attachments and interpersonal relationships.

The human brain is designed to be social and relate to others. Writers in the disciplines of interpersonal neurobiology, **attachment** and child development (Cozolino, 2006, 2014; Music, 2017; Panksepp, 1998; Siegel, 2012a, 2012b) cover these areas in depth, and so I reflect back to these theories within the material in the book; however, I am not going to explain all the concepts in depth. I will show you the how, what and why, and of course, the ultimate aim of this book is how to help children, young people and perhaps even adults when needed.

This book is primarily about human beings and the relationships they have with each other in cyberspace. However, to understand what happens in cyberspace also known as 'online' I am beginning this book with what happens in real-world life (outside of this space) known as the **corporeal** so that the reader can take this knowledge and see how this applies to the online world, because it's the same yet different.

In order to understand why we communicate as we do and why we need to relate to other people in order to get our needs met (i.e. to be fulfilled or to receive love, care and understanding from another person without any conditions attached to it), we need to learn about how babies do this and how they form relationships as the foundation of this entire book. I will keep coming back to these very basic drives and behaviours. That means I have to introduce you, the reader, to **attachment theory** which was initially proposed by John Bowlby (1969, as cited in Bowlby, 1997) before we discuss the online world. So, let's start at the beginning, a great place to journey from.

A point to note about my approach and perspective in terms of understanding human relationships comes from synthesising an approach called attachment theory with neuroscience (an overarching approach, not just 'the brain'). The reason I would like you as the reader to become familiar with it is because of the following:

A   I'll be referring to these ideas a lot and you ought to know what I am talking about. I will keep talking about the styles/types of attachment throughout, and I don't want to lose you with this language.

B   Attachment theory was considered to not be a "real" science as it was first developed yet has stood the test of time as a theory that supports many of the behaviours of human beings.

C   I will be talking to you about being a good enough parent/professional and not the 'perfect' one that often appears in books or on TV shows. This is because 'good enough' attachments help build a resilient mind, brain and body that enables children to manage times of distress and to regulate their emotions in relation to this distress. Perfection can lead to burnout, and this book is here to help you achieve a balanced view and approach and not to attack your parenting/caring style. This is about empowering you, and in order to do that, I leave the expertise up to you. I show you the research and you decide what's best for your/the child, family and situation.

D   Technology has helped us understand complex theories. I will combine how we use technology, and I will introduce you to these concepts and behaviours as we go along. The advances in science, technology and understanding the human body/brain are remarkable and exciting, and we are the humans who 'interface' with this technology. This interaction with or around technology has an implication and effect on our behaviour and biology and vice versa. Hopefully, by the end of this book, you will be able to understand your child better and have an understanding of what is happening in their minds, brains and bodies, too, in relation to the technological and digital world.

E   Attachment underpins my propositions in this book and will help you see why we do what we do online (and in real life) and can give you a rounded overview of your child and not one driven by panic, misrepresented science in the news or scaremongering from people who do not have a broad understanding of human behaviour. It always helps the parents whom I'm supporting when I'm able to say this isn't my science, nor am I making this up, and in terms of what the academics write about, often in narrow fields of human behaviour, this is a *whole-istic* way of understanding your child. (I purposefully use this spelling compared to *holistic* as you can see what I'm getting at).

To be understood is all many of us really want, need, desire and deserve. I am bringing you the book to help you do just that.

Catherine Knibbs

References

Bowlby, J. (1997). *Attachment and loss* (2nd ed.). Pimlico.

Cozolino, L. (2006). *The neuroscience of human relationships: Attachment and the developing social brain* (1st ed.). WW Norton & Co.

Cozolino, L. (2014). *The neuroscience of human relationships: Attachment and the developing social brain* (2nd ed.). WW Norton & Co.

Music, G. (2017). *Nurturing natures. Attachment and children's emotional, sociocultural and brain development* (2nd ed.). Routledge.

Panksepp, J. (1998). *Affective neuroscience. The foundations of human and animal emotions.* Oxford University Press.

Siegel, D. (2012a). *The developing mind. How relationships and the brain interact to shape who we are.* WW Norton & Co.

Siegel, D. (2012b). *The pocket guide to interpersonal neurobiology. An integrative handbook of the mind.* WW Norton & Co.

Section I

The theory of human development in a world of technology

Attachment, trauma and child development in an exponential technological age

1 Attachment and infancy

The foundation of our behaviour and development

Introduction
Technology and children; the developing child in a cyberspace womb?

There are many children who are now forever captured in cyberspace in their 'scan pictures', for which they had no say in being shared via social media channels. For example, parents may share the picture of their developing baby online, and in doing so, what would be the ethical implication if it turned out a professional 'read' that picture and detected an abnormality in the image that could have an effect on the child's health in later life? Would the professional be duty-bound to say something? Would the child have agreed or consented to it being shared in this way? I don't know the answer to either of these questions and some presented here throughout the book, and whose decision, ethics, morals or values is it anyway? Again, this can be an ethical dilemma for some of us and may need much more thought about when/how/why we share pictures in this way. Most cases of sharing these pictures have a simple explanation: these parents want to proudly announce the impending arrival and success of their fertility (because this is what we do in real life). Rather than waiting for the visible bump to be the initiator of that conversation (because that can take months), we tell people, usually appearing like proud, puffed-up peacocks. Pride is a drive for conversation. We are proud of our reproductive skills and often wish to celebrate with our family, village or tribe.

However, we can sometimes forget that not every human can procreate, and through our sharing of our news, this can be terribly difficult for some to see or hear, especially if they have lost children too. It's certainly not to say that we shouldn't share our news with our friends, on- and offline. And herein lies an early question for us in this book: if we forget/don't/won't consider the implications of our behaviours online as adults

DOI: 10.4324/9781003169390-2

because we are excited, proud, angry (or add in any emotions you feel), why would, should or how can a child?

Babies

So perhaps let's start with newborns. I'm going to invite you to imagine a picture of a baby; this may be one you already know. I'd like to invite you to think about what newborns do? That probably didn't take long as I'm sure your answer was limited to a small number of bodily functions. However, I'm going to discuss what infants do, and I'll put these into a small list here as we come back to the important factors for this book.

Babies, immediately after birth, seek the face of a person (although their eyes are not very sharp in perception/focus immediately after birth, and I will cover blind/partially sighted babies in a moment). This face is usually the mother whom the baby is placed with after birth. They can focus (although it is blurry to begin with) at approximately 30 to 40 cm, which is almost the same distance from face to breast, so babies look towards Mum whilst breastfeeding and 'imprint' her face and feelings of safety into **implicit** memory (without words). They feel her heartbeat, feel the warmth of her skin/touch and, more than likely, hear her voice in this space too. This (face-)seeking attachment behaviour is biologically innate (primal) and strong. This survival instinct is so powerful that it does not need any 'programming' for it to take place. It looks the same, even with children who are born without sight who react to their mother's voices and orientate towards their face, with researchers finding that infants who are blind seem to present the same characteristics of attachment (Demir et al., 2014; Fraiberg, 1977; Werth, 1984). It is much more complex than this, obviously, for children without sight; however, I am highlighting the power of attachment here primarily. We have no conscious control over our primal **bio-survival circuitry**, so we humans follow biology first and foremost. Alongside this process, there is what Porges (2011) calls a **neural expectation**, which means that as the infant looks towards the mother, there is an expectation that the mother will also look directly back at the infant. When this does not occur, a feeling of stress is encountered, and the infant may well then engage other communication processes, such as making a noise or reacting with their body. To give you an example of this, have you ever smiled at someone and, in return, they scowl or look blankly past you? Did you notice how your body reacted instantaneously and created a feeling or thought of 'What did I do wrong?' or 'Why are they ignoring me?' and one remark we often can say when we are telling someone else about being ignored is 'How rude!' (the ignorer was). This is your nervous system and brain working together in the **social engagement system** process whereby, by default, there is this 'expectation' of the rules of reciprocal communication which we implicitly know: I smile; you smile.

Babies also turn towards certain sounds, such as mum's voice and changes in their visual periphery (e.g. flashes of light/movement). Babies turn their heads towards these stimuli and away from visuals/sounds that are overstimulating/loud. A new and novel (not-too-loud) noise or light causes the **orienting response** to be triggered (Marios et al., 1983), and here the baby will look towards the sight/sound, an important fact that we will return to later. However, the regularity of the stimuli (sound) results in what is called habituation. (It loses its novelty.) Therefore, you may have seen doctors clap near newborns to assess whether they can hear.

Like temperature control, babies cannot regulate many of their bodily responses in the first few months, such as shivering, management of their feelings, toileting habits or hunger, and need help do these things. If a noise is frightening and makes the baby jump or if they feel scared, overwhelmed, hungry, wet, cold, warm, irritated, in pain, lonely, fed up, tired and so on, they will communicate this to the people around them. This concept of protesting this uncontrollable feeling means they are *requesting regulation*. For example, think of a thermostat that controls your heating; babies and many children and young people need you to be their emotional thermostat until they can do this for themselves. This might just be until they are in their 20s. Yes, their 20s! This is called **Emotional regulation** and is perhaps the most important aspect in terms of attachment and what we will discuss in this book in the how to help sections.

Babies, in general, do not have a regular sleep pattern in the first few weeks or months. They can't tell the difference between night and day (to begin with). To keep this brief, I explain this is because they have been in an environment for 9 months where it was always dark. Babies' brains need to learn the difference between light and dark, and the part of the brain that controls this is learning with each day too. This is called the **circadian rhythm** and is controlled by light passing through the eyes to the light receptors at the back of the eye which then tell the pineal gland in the brain to make a hormone called melatonin, which makes us sleepy when it gets dark (Panda, 2018).

Also, babies can generally only stay awake for small amounts of time before the brain gets fatigued from all the new learning and because of the brain state it operates in (more on this later). The way we consolidate information, memory and learning is through sleep (this will also be important when we get to adolescents and how to help).

Babies learn without words. It has been said that babies are born blank slates, and I don't personally or professionally agree with this. I do agree, however, that they learn a set of patterns based on what happens in their environment. Babies need to learn about their role and their environment, and to do this they rely on repetitive patterns of behaviours. Their brains are highly open to learning new things every day, and repetition is a way to consolidate this. If they can create an automatic memory of these everyday occurrences called a 'schema', this helps them focus on the new stuff, as the brain creates a shortcut to stop focusing on this aspect, like when they learn to crawl or walk. It's a bit like learning to tie your shoelace; it requires a lot of concentration at the beginning until you know how to do it, and then you don't concentrate on it at all really.

Babies create an invisible attachment to their caregivers, who are usually Mum and Dad primarily (I use the academic term *primary caregiver* to mean these people) and then bond with other people such as siblings, grandparents and extended family members. As babies are born, they cannot control their body temperature, crawl or walk within the first few hours like other baby mammals, so they needed to develop other strategies to survive. If you think for a moment, what babies do is very clever and works a treat, and it is not manipulation. It is survival of the cutest/loudest/quietest, whatever works for this child in this family. They have a very loud cry (protest), and they have facial features that make you feel like you want to help, such as big eyes and soft round cheeks. Most babies are adorable, and to their parents, they say they are the most beautiful people on the planet. And they need to be to recruit their parents into caring for them! Evolution is very wise and clever. This is also one of the reasons we find baby animals so cute. It's an invisible mechanism in our brains that almost magnetically pulls us towards an infant to take care of it. Now maybe the kitten and puppy pictures on the internet make sense as to why we like them so much. And maybe kittens are indeed like the cutest things ever?

This brings me to the type of care an infant receives and the feelings/attachment story (without words) they tell themselves about who they are and who cares for them and makes them feel safe. I know babies can't speak; however, they are able to understand routines, the people in those routines and the feelings associated with those routines, and these result in what we academics call an attachment style. I will reiterate this part of the book is really important in terms of how I will describe online behaviours so having an understanding of how infants make sense of the world you can see how older children and adults make sense of their world both online and with other people.

For you to understand the differences in attachments styles, I'm going to tell four short stories. These will be slightly exaggerated, so you can understand the differences; however, in my line of work, these are not necessarily untrue events, and children do have/had these experiences. As a cautionary word, I discuss things that may be uncomfortable to read and may jiggle an old memory or feeling for you. This is where I suggest that you read at your pace and, if need be, take that self-care break.

As I have no control over who reads this book, I emphasise the self-care suggestion as readers may be affected by the content within the book. Although it is my intention to educate, I am aware and sensitive to the fact that this content can take you back in time to moments of your past. If this happens, please do what you need to take care of yourself.

Attachment

The following stories talk about lanes of traffic (on a motorway/freeway) with colours denoted to these lanes. This is based on my explanations to children and families in my clinic, where I also created content on my website to reflect these in relation to stress and **trauma** (Knibbs, 2019). To make this as easy as possible for you to understand, think of a motorway (freeway in the US) that has three lanes. The middle lane is green, and the outer lanes are red and blue, respectively.

Story 1 takes place in the green lane: I'm going to talk about a child who has a picturesque home and parents. They live in Disney-made-up land where everyone has a wonderful home, enough money for food, holidays and there is harmony with their neighbours; they have cats, dogs, horses and plenty of space to roam, and everyone is healthy. In this city lives a family. Let's call the child Susie and her parents Lola and Joshua.

Susie was a planned pregnancy and one during which Lola was able to take a large amount of maternity leave and could potter around her home getting ready for Susie's arrival while feeling comfortable and relaxed. Joshua worked hard, and when he came home, he supported Lola, and they decided to have a home birth with the help of a doula. The birth was very calm and serene, and Susie was born without any complications. Susie was placed on Lola's chest, and they were left to bond for as long as was needed. In this time, Lola and Joshua marvelled with many ooohs and ahhhs at Susie's arrival, and she was held, cuddled and breastfed when she was ready.

Lola and Joshua understood the developments in brain science and knew that they could help Susie develop by connecting with her at her pace in what's called an **attuned** regulation or 'serve and return' pattern.

They learned facts about Susie's communication and knew when Susie turned her head away this was Susie's communication of 'I've had enough of this', and her parents would respect this fact and wait for Susie's signal of permission and readiness for them to return to communicating with her. They talked in motherese (like a sing-song voice), sang to her, massaged her and told her how she was loved, wanted and adored even though they knew she may not understand the words but that she would understand the intention behind them. They also picked her up when she cried because they understood that being left alone when crying was detrimental to her emotional regulation skills. They knew if they left her to 'cry it out' too often, this would result in something called toxic stress and avoided it where they could, whilst also being compassionate with their selves to know that *100% attuned emotional regulation is not possible for any parent.* They attended to her needs and understood that they were the 'grown-ups' and that they had to be her regulator of emotions, schedule, temperature and her internal story of "I am safe and secure with my parents".

Susie was a securely attached infant and she knew this deep down to her core. She felt it and knew her parents were reliable and would help her manage any distress she felt now and in the future. She also knew that she was going to be okay and to be able to manage tolerable distress by herself when it arose and that she could use her parents to help her manage when this became too much to bear. Susie was cared for like this all the way through her childhood. In terms of a phrase that is appearing more and more in health and education Susie would be called resilient. I am going to add that this may be called *secure resilient.*

Stories 2, 3 and 4 are not so picturesque and perfect, and these are the children we mostly concentrate on throughout this book. As before, these stories are fictional but based on real children who have appeared in my practice. All identifying information has been removed or changed.

Story 2 takes place in the blue lane. Peter was a planned pregnancy; however, when Julie, his mum, was halfway through the pregnancy, she broke up with her partner, Daniel. Peter was born slightly early at 37 weeks, and Mum was both happy to see Peter and very frantically worried about how she would cope as a single parent. Julie managed to arrange with Daniel that he would come over to help look after Peter so he had a part in his life.

When Daniel was not there, Julie would struggle to meet the demands of Peter, and he would often be left crying as Julie would find herself in distress and not know what to do. She would get irritated with Peter and would jerkily lift him from his cot and bounce him quite hard whilst muttering that he was a demanding baby and that it was too hard for her to cope. She would try to breastfeed Peter and he would turn his head away, and Julie would swap him to the other breast and tell him he must feed now because she didn't have time later when the TV soaps were on. If Peter was in his bouncy chair, Julie would often stare past him at the TV and on occasions forgot he was there and trip over the bouncy chair.

When Daniel arrived, he would spend time chatting with Julie. Peter would be in his bouncy chair in front of them and he would be ignored. Peter gurgled and cooed to them to no avail. Sometimes, Daniel would tell him to "just shut up" if he and Julie were talking or watching a film. Peter was sometimes left with a wet and dirty nappy for hours. As Peter began to develop and could hold his own bottle, both Julie and Daniel would force it into his mouth and tell him to drink it. When he was mastering the art of holding it up with his little arms, they would take it off him or hold it on an angle that seemed to create discomfort for Peter. If Peter was crawling, they would pick him up and sit him in front of the item he was crawling towards as he was 'getting in their way' or 'taking too long'.

Daniel often missed the days he said he would come around after a few months and Julie was mainly on her own with Peter. She became cross and irritated with him and now began to leave him alone in his chair or cot for longer periods of time. Peter began to quieten down and did not cry or make noises when he was hungry, wet or needed attention. Peter also didn't seem to react to Mum's shouting or muttering, and he would often look rather limp and uninterested. People would comment what a good baby he was when he was out in the pram as he made no noises and didn't seem like a "fussy" baby. Peter has what is known as *(anxious-) avoidant attachment.*

Peter avoids asking for his needs to be met: attention, hunger satisfying or human connection and cuddles. Peter has experienced parents who avoided connecting with him and rejoicing in him. Peter had an experience of not being accepted for all his feelings, and now he avoids them because they bring him deep pain of rejection, emptiness and loneliness. Peter has decided in his story of the world that 'he will become independent and do things by himself; he will stay away from people as they bring unwanted feelings. He will reject, deny and avoid people; this will keep him safe'. This is his survival mechanism and script, and he will defend it to the nth degree, denying or playing down that he does this.

Story 3 takes place in the red lane. Alice was a planned pregnancy to begin with. Around 12 weeks into the pregnancy her mum, Maggie, became anxious about the baby and her abilities as a mum and considered an abortion. She changed her mind again about a fortnight later. This continued and included discussions about giving her up for adoption and keeping her until the day Alice was born. Alice was born slightly late at 41 weeks and was a difficult birth, with lots of people telling Maggie what to do and Maggie felt very confused during this time.

When Alice was born, Maggie tried to breastfeed but couldn't manage it and so asked the nurse for a bottle. Maggie then tried breastfeeding again and bottle-feeding. By the end of the first week, Maggie had given up trying to breastfeed Alice. Maggie was cross that Alice would not feed this way and felt herself a failure and would discuss this often when family came to visit. Maggie found it daunting to look after Alice and would ask her partner, John, to help during the nights, but he would say he was tired; sometimes he would go to see Alice and feed/settle/change her, and other times, he wouldn't. Alice was sometimes left with a wet nappy for hours, and other times she was changed quickly by her parents, and it seemed to be dependent on how busy/tired they said they were.

Some evenings, John would sit with Alice, and he would sing to her and read her a book (even though she didn't understand the words), and other nights, he would take her to her cot and put her in and leave her there without speaking to say good night. Maggie would sometimes do the same. Maggie would also be sharp with Alice and sometimes would be quite rough when changing her, pulling her legs back hard and being irritated with her, and, other times, would laugh along with Alice and play along with her wriggles. When Alice was in her pram, she would smile at strangers on some occasions, or she would scream at the same person the day after. Alice has what is called an *(anxious-)ambivalent attachment* style.

Alice was often confused about whether she should ask for her needs to be met, so sometimes, she would begin to cry and then go quiet or would almost scream the house down and make herself so loud and noticeable. She was what people call "clingy and whiney" or "moody" and would push other children/people out of the picture, such as when John was talking to Maggie, she would cry until Maggie picked her up, even if Maggie was irritated with her, and pulled her onto her knee, hurting Alice in the process.

Alice developed a story of 'I'm unworthy and have to compete for my needs to be met and I need attention constantly to feel safe as being ignored leaves me feeling confused about whether you will ever come back. I need to recruit you to look after me and to hold me centre stage, and sometimes, I may ask for more love and attention than you can give. I also need my own autonomy and get cross when you help/interfere. I am unsure about how safe I am and need constant reassurances'. This survival mechanism would see her through life by being both in need and independent. People around her will not always know what she wants or how to be with her consistently. She will both defend this and ask for help to change, never fully committing to either. Her narrative will seem as though the events of her past are the things that control her present, and she will talk about the past quite often.

Story 4 takes place erratically between the blue and red lanes. Robert was an unplanned and unwanted pregnancy, and both his parents, Lucy and Gary, were quite young when Lucy became pregnant. They were both religious and decided that they would keep the baby. Due to finances, they lived with Gary's parents as Lucy's parents were alcoholics and drug users and had kicked her out of the house for being pregnant. Whilst Lucy was pregnant, there was a lot of shouting and fighting at Gary's parents due to Lucy's parents turning up and arguing with people in the street and house. Gary and his parents also often screamed and shouted at each other in the house or street, and the police would often make an appearance. Lucy would run to the bathroom when this was happening, and she and Gary would then argue. It was a volatile environment for everyone. Lucy gave birth to Robert at home prematurely around 36 weeks and had to be rushed to hospital because of complications. When she was there, her parents turned up and offered for her to return to the family home. They promised they would change their habits now that Robert had been born. Lucy moved back with her parents.

Robert would often hear his grandparents, who, being drunk most nights of the week, shouted and argued with each other, or the TV was loud. Visitors to the house, such as neighbours, were also very loud, and it made it difficult for Robert to settle and go to sleep. He became difficult to calm/soothe, or he would be difficult to wake for feeds. Lucy would often get into arguments about the lack of food in the cupboards and there being no money for food. Sometimes, she would be holding Robert when this happened. When she was angry, she would bang the doors and go back to her room with Robert. When she was there, she would sing to him and tell him things are going to be okay. On occasions, Lucy would lose her temper with Robert for no apparent reason, and she would also shout at him and was very rough when changing his nappy, even on one occasion smacking his thighs. Gary would visit irregularly, and he and Lucy would argue verbally, and on some occasions, they would be physically aggressive with each other whilst Robert was in the room. Robert spent much time during his first few months of life frozen in fear or crying loudly. Robert seemed terrified of people and animals when out in his pram; at times, he would cry, and other times, he seemed to stare into the sky and not even blink. Robert has what is called a *disorganised attachment* style.

Robert's story about the world is 'no one is safe and those who are supposed to protect you are the causes of the fear you feel. Do not trust anyone and look after yourself. Show no fear and perhaps at times be violent with others to keep yourself safe and free from any relationships because they are dangerous. If they show you any care, they are likely to be tricking you and can become dangerous at any moment. I want to be close and have real connecting relationships with people but don't know how. I will recruit you to look after me (helplessness), but I will reject you to keep myself safe. I can also do this to myself and dissociate away from the here and now' (almost like daydreaming).

★This is not an exercise for self-diagnosis as you would need to do this with a qualified therapist who works with attachment.

These attachment styles are the way in which we can understand a child and their attempts to make sense of the world. As you can see the attachment styles appear in the lanes that accompany the preceding stories. In reality, it is more complicated than this as babies, children and adults can have a mixture of attachment styles, for certain people, which is why you may have heard phrases like 'She's never like that for me', or 'Why does he always play up for me?' If we stay in one lane for a long time, particularly in childhood, it can become our dominant way of relating to people when under stress.

In summary, the attachment styles are secure (green lane), avoidant (blue lane), ambivalent (red lane) and disorganised (blue/red lanes). These attachment patterns form our "subconscious and unconscious operating system to the world of human relationships". We do not actually possess an operating system like iOS or Windows, but the emphasis is on our automatic patterns of bonding with another person that we are unaware of.

References

Demir, T., Bolat, N., Yavuz, M., Karacetin, G., Dogangun, B., & Kayaalp, L. (2014). Attachment characteristics and behavioural problems in children and adolescents with congenital blindness. *Archives of Neuropsychiatry, 51*, 116–121. https://doi.org/10.1023/A:1025349908855

Fraiberg, S., & Frailberg, L. (1977). *Insights from the blind: Comparative studies of blind and sighted infants.* Basic Books.

Knibbs, C. (2019). www.catherineknibbs.co.uk

Marios, A., Labonte, K., Parent, M., & Vachon, F. (1983). Eyes have ears: Indexing the orienting response to sound using pupillometry. *International Journal of Psychophysiology, 123*, 152–162. https://doi.org/10.1016/j.ijpsycho.2017.09.016

Panda, S. (2018). *The circadian code.* Penguin Random House.

Porges, S. (2011). *The polyvagal theory. Neurophysiological foundations of emotions, attachment, communication and self-regulation.* WW Norton & Co.

Werth, L. (1984). Syncrony of cueing modalities: Communicative competence between the mother and blind infant. *Early Child Development and Care, 18*(1–2), 53–60. doi:10.1080/0300443840180103

2 Trauma

A very basic introduction

Introduction

In the previous chapter, I have drip-fed some child trauma events into the stories to enable us to layer the next perspective of development and issues children face. The online space brings many of these to the forefront. *Trauma* is an interesting word to consider. Again, the English lexicon (dictionary) and semantics (meanings) don't do the word justice. I often teach about trauma having more than one meaning. In the medical community, it refers to the size, depth and seriousness of a wound or injury. In the psychological literature, it refers to an event, both natural and unnatural such as an earthquake (natural), falling off a bike (accident), physical/sexual/emotional assault (intentional) or the lack of survival support (neglect). However, in terms of trauma theory, it is the story of 'what happened to me, and how I (mind, brain and body) have made sense of it'. It is an internal narrative which is nonverbal, and the use of external language to coherently understand. Therefore, that makes *trauma* both a noun and verb. In common everyday language, it can mean something serious such as or a drama or perhaps even an exaggeration of an event; for example young people may say that something is traumatic when they do not necessarily mean any of the above. This does not negate their experience; however, as we move through the book, the word *trauma* is considered something that has a negative impact that does not necessarily result in something called post-traumatic stress.

To understand trauma, there is a requirement to see the impact it has on our biology, brains, minds and bodies. Unfortunately, for most parents, teachers and professionals, when they speak with those of us who work with it clinically, they can find that we often use lots of scientific, anatomic and medical names without considering the non–#neuro nerds out there or those who do not care for the science. So, I'm going to tell you another story. I will introduce some of the brain areas to you as we go

DOI: 10.4324/9781003169390-3

along in this story, and before you know, you'll understand the metaphor of how we work.

Evolution theory has taught us a lot about how we have evolved. In terms of our brains, they simply have not changed much since the time of Neanderthals, and our behaviour in 2020 would reflect that of a caveman/woman should they be placed in your local town/city. (No joke!) Our brain is said to be made up of three parts that look like they sit on top of each other and connect with each other from top to bottom. You may have read that we have two sides of our brains also and that these are used for different functions. This is a very simple version and one that helps us talk about what is happening in a generic way. However, the brain is much more complex than this, and to understand trauma, I must go a little deeper in explaining here; don't worry, though, I intend to keep it simple.

This brings me to my academic disclaimer: I am aware that the brain is a differentiated and complex organ and one which cannot be reduced to its component parts, and I do not intend to convey this through these writings; however, this is a book for parents and professionals with no formal education around neuroscience and biology. However, I intend to honour the implicit understanding that parents and professionals have. To do this, I use examples from books already written on the brain and use examples where possible to expand the understanding for you.

I'm going to use and expand on an example from Drs Dan Siegel and Tina Bryson (2012), who refer their readers to the brain as a *metaphor of a house* (It is not 'set out' like this, it is a way for you to understand without Neuroscience training). There is an upstairs and downstairs and a left and right. Every part of the house has something or someone in it, and there are jobs for these things/people to do. In the downstairs part of the brain, no one talks with words, and in the upstairs part, everyone talks. I'd like to introduce you to the occupants of the house and point out some of the occupants who arrive/begin to speak at varying times throughout a child's/adolescent's development. (These are not 'real' people, animals or things by the way, again, a metaphor to understand.)

The downstairs part of the brain is made up of two basic, but highly effective, areas. The one closest to the front door we will call the reptilian area, and the other part just behind it we will call the mammalian area. These operate most of our bodily functions in the background, and we do not have verbal access to these parts. (A bit like trying to explain how you know how to walk/run/catch/ride a bike). Information passes through the front door and may pass through this area to the upstairs, but not always. There is a command centre that sits just behind the doorway with a big red button. This button controls the autonomic nervous system response activation.

The reptilian area behaves exactly as its name denotes, and if you have ever watched a gecko, they don't talk and pretty much do the same thing every day which is to follow the 3 Fs of survival of the species, which are to feed, fear (prey/being eaten) and fornicate (of course, this is the F you thought of?) This area is also concerned with controlling our Bs – breathing, balance, beating heart, body temperature and bedtime (circadian rhythm) – as well as the Fs. Behind the reptilian area sits the mammalian system which behaves like, let's say, a puppy. Again, this area does not have words, and this area is concerned with the Fs, the Bs and the Ms, which are, memories and motivations (for survival/safety) and (e)-motions arising. This area makes decisions based on the incoming information and is assessed by two Amys (L and R **amygdala**) that sit here and rate the information as familiar or not.

The Amys are a little bit like the Health and Safety or Ofsted (the Office of Standards in Education, Childrens Services and Skills in the UK) team that decides how dangerous, risky or life-threatening something is. They often communicate with the downstairs residents to ensure they have assessed the information correctly. They have been known to get mixed up on occasions or be given false information. When this happens or the information is unfamiliar, they often press the red button 'just in case'. This button sets off a stress response in the house, which we can call the survival or react to the environment response, and this overrides all other processes in the house when pressed. Now I am not entirely sure that Joseph Le-Doux (2002, 2015) ever explained the **amygdala** in this way, and having seen many books and people talking about this area being the 'fear centre of the brain', I want to emphasise the way this area works in a way that makes sense to people and to move away from this narrative.

Amy R tends to press the red button most often and, as such, can be a bit overprotective, anxious and reactive yet does this with the best of intentions. She operates on a 'better safe than sorry' and 'err on the side of caution' approach. This can often result in Amy R becoming very 'jumpy' or 'hyper-vigilant soldier on duty'. Downstairs is our safety and survival system (which includes attachment behaviours).

Upstairs is made up of residents who are older/wiser men and women, mathematicians, time-travelling storytellers, doctors, artists, mime experts, magicians (mind readers), judges, health and safety inspectors, athletes, music conductors/composers, computer operators, referees, teachers, memory experts, chess-like champions, a coach or two, a gym instructor and a wise old guru. Upstairs is a very busy place by the time a person gets to 25 years of age. Most of the occupants talk, and many tend to collect at the front of the house; it can get a bit squashed and noisy at times!

An important fact to take note of here is the information from the front door takes about 0.3 to 0.5 seconds to arrive upstairs. You might have worked out that the reptile/mammalian parts of the brain often make decisions before the upstairs has time to understand (assimilate) what's happening. The upstairs part of the brain must try to make sense of what happened a moment ago and in what order, and therefore, we can make often up stories about what we 'think' happened. In effect, we are 0.5 seconds behind everything we do and that makes us permanent time-travellers, perhaps?

The upstairs 'thinking' part of the brain is where most of our 'rational' and 'cognitive' work takes place, and it makes sense (as best it can) of the information that the downstairs part of the brain is communicating. It is easily knocked 'off-line' by head injuries, substances, anaesthetic and, important for us here, the emotions/feelings becoming 'too big'. If the big red alarm button is pressed, it can be too noisy and overwhelming for us to think and make sense of things happening in that moment. The upstairs area can become disorientated or confused and cannot think for all the noise and commotion. It takes time for things to calm down. The upstairs is our thinking system called 'executive functioning' (Siegel, 2012).

Each person on the planet has a house which is built with the same plans (blueprint) and contains most of the same occupants when optimal conditions are provided; however, each person's house looks different from everyone else's. The occupants arrive at different stages at each person's house during their development (even in twins, triplets and beyond). It depends on what happens to that person as they grow and what experiences they have as to 'who shows up and when' in the house and what the environment is like that the brain is in during its development. Now obviously we don't actually have these people and things in our brain like this; however, to make neuroscience accessible for you, I have designated differentiated parts of the brain as characters so that I can reference these within the book.

The brain is a collection of 'cells' rather like you have in your body. When cells have optimal environments to thrive in, they grow and communicate with each other easily. If the cells are surrounded by toxic elements, they retreat from this and do not grow but stay in 'protect and defend mode'. They do not communicate very well with other cells. This toxicity is what we often refer to as child abuse, neglect and trauma and even consists of societal pressures, issues, economics and force majeure. Take for example our collective responses to COVID-19 in 2020; we retreated to stay safe.

And now a story using the house metaphor to illustrate trauma and how the brain and body work together. First, there are three pathways to the front door of the house. Each time a messenger arrives at the house from a path, they bring information that relates to the person's internal and external environment such as intestines, stomach, genitals, heart, lungs, vocal cords and even facial muscles. Sometimes the messages brought relate to the senses of taste, touch, sight, sound and smell. When the messenger carries a message away from the house, it goes to a place in the body, for example the stomach or muscles to make the person move.

When a message arrives at the 'front door', it is only heard by the downstairs part of the house to begin with. The upstairs part only becomes aware when needed (or about half a second later). This is done to save time, energy and resources. Imagine how busy we would be if we had to listen out for and count every heartbeat, breath and movement in your intestines as well as think about the things we have to think about!

However, Amy R can often overhear the messages at the front door as she is very nosy and feels it's her job to listen in to them. She feels she was handed this job by our ancestors, the Neanderthals, and is very proud and takes the job seriously. She is so proud of her job that she can be overly helpful and, without a moment's thought, presses the red panic button if she feels the house, the messengers or the body needs protection from a perceived threat. She is keen to be the best at her job and doesn't always learn quickly either; she has been known to press the panic button for the same message just because she recognises the messenger and makes an assumption about 'knowing what the message is in advance'. I'm sure you know people like this in your life too.

Amy R often misunderstands what a threat is, she often is not thinking carefully or logically about the message or situation, she's almost a 'react and ask questions later!' kind of girl. This is an innate survival skill we all have, and Amy R can be a little 'jumpy' at times. If you know anyone who is always 'on the lookout for danger' or 'worries' (i.e. anxious), this is a reason why. Amy R's biological name is the amygdala. The job of a good psychotherapist is to be what Louis Cozolino (2006) calls an 'amygdala whisperer', and this isn't as simple as whispering to Amy R; I can tell you, she is very set in her ways, and it can take a lot of time, patience and compassionate work to help her learn that the world can be safe.

Stories to illustrate the processes

Louise was born and regulated in the green lanes. Louise is born to parents who attune (resonate) with her and play lots of baby games like peekaboo and sing nursery rhymes. One day, a messenger runs up one of the paths and gives a message to her. This message is 'My tummy is empty and needs filling', which we as adults know and call the feeling of hunger. The messenger now takes this information to her vocal cords, and she makes a crying sound. Her parents come to her very quickly, and they nourish and feed her. The tummy (hunger) message changes to a new message of 'I am satisfied'. This feeling travels around her body, and Louise appears content and happy to her parents, so they hold her gently whilst she snuggles into them feeling all warm and fuzzy. All is well and peaceful in her internal 'house'. The upstairs part of the house who have been watching this process decide that this is a story of "I cry, and Mummy/Daddy will come to me quickly and I will have my needs met, and I trust this is how it will always be". They put this feeling story into her (attachment) 'script' memory box. For each need Louise has, her messengers work well and in harmony with one another, and her parents decode each noise, facial expressions and body movement to help Louise's house stay calm and well regulated. Her "attachment script" memory box is filling up with lots of secure messages about how life is safe: she is seen by her parents; she is secure and soothed when she feels dysregulated. This almost sounds too good to be true, doesn't it? That a baby is always attuned to and regulated? Truth be told, this is highly unlikely as parents are not always at hand, not always available to attune because let's face it, we have lots going on and babies can be difficult to understand for the first few weeks or months. However, this story is for illustration about the 'good enough approach', whereby we can do our best to be good enough and not perfect. I see many parents in therapy who attempt to achieve this 'perfection', most likely due to pressures from other parents (grandparents), health care professionals and, nowadays, social media, and it's exhausting, because it's impossible. Good enough is good enough. Please do use this sentence as permission to allow you to 'go easy on yourself' from trying to achieve perfection.

Michael, born and regulated in the green lane, is moved to the blue lane by a life event. Michael is born to parents who attune to him and play lots of baby like games like peekaboo and the dance of the nappy change. One day, Michael is asleep in the car with his parents when there is a minor car accident. Nobody is hurt in the collision, but it is an abrupt 'shock' to everyone. The messengers from his body rush up to the house, all at once, and try to push in with their message; they are shouting to be heard and speaking very fast because they have to alert the brain to this sudden event. It could be a life-or-death situation, and it's mayhem! The gecko/puppy in the doorway tries to understand the hubbub; meanwhile, Amy R says no messing and hits the red alarm button. The result is everyone is flustered and forgets to send a signal to the vocal cords to alert his parents to his distress! On the outside looking in, Michael is very silent, very still, and it looks like maybe he's "not bothered". His parents are very frantic and are speaking at him rather than to him; however, the messengers and downstairs part of the house can't understand and can't hear anything because of the alarm going off. Michael's body is so overwhelmed by all this noise and hustle and bustle that his body decides to go limp to try to conserve his energy. It's all very disjointed and confused.

However, after a few seconds, the alarm is turned off as Amy R realises that the danger has passed (it's actually the occupants of upstairs who tell her this as they can see out of the windows and see that Mum and Dad are talking to Michael); everyone takes a deep breath and begins to decipher/ hear the messages of his parents' voices and the system 'resets'. All the incoming information from the body is beginning to make more sense, each messenger takes their turn to speak and it's less noisy and chaotic. The return messages to the body are to 'calm down'. Michael's mum is now holding him and talking to him in a slow, rhythmic way, telling him that it will all be okay and that it was a shocking moment for all of them. His parents carry on talking to him and reassuring him, and his messengers begin to arrive at the front door with messages that reflect the now-calming parts of his body. The downstairs part of the house now communicates more effectively with the upstairs part of the house which says, 'Okay, all clear; things are returning to the settled state'. It was a bit of a moment!

Later that day, Michaels parents show him what happened by playing with toy cars in front of him with his teddies, and they show him that when there was the bump of the cars, people were shocked and how they came to him and held him and rocked him. Although Michael is too young to fully understand the story in the way an adult would, the way his parents reflected this event to him help him feel safe as he watches a third-person account of the day's events. Children can often make sense of an event when it is replayed in this way so that it is a story of 'what happened to me', and this is why children can re-enact scenes of terror and distress in this way, attempting to make sense of them.

Disclaimer: This is not always an intervention or activity to use with all children for all events; please use your discretion as very traumatic events do not benefit from this 'storytelling mode' without the help of a well-trained professional. Seek the advice of a professional trained in/ around trauma for direction around life stories and issues.

To understand how trauma can take time to integrate, I will elaborate on the rest of Michael's day to show you that the body remembers and how this can be seen in a story like this:

> When Michael is put to bed that night and the light is turned out one of the messengers runs up the path to the house and shouts, 'It's

all gone dark like earlier today it must be another crash happening again!!' For a moment, the alarms are sounded because we know Amy R is alert to this and still a bit jittery and prone to pressing the button. Michael becomes restless in his cot, and a little tearful, he is whimpering but not crying as his messengers are a little confused but not overwhelmingly scared. The upstairs occupants who have worked out what is going at this point shout down to Amy R, 'Stop! It's not the same thing; this is night-time, we do this at the end of every day, this is familiar, it's all okay, but thank you for being on high alert. We need you to do your job and alert us when there is real danger'. One of the upstairs occupants is a very wise guru and knows that this darkness is due to night-time routines and not the car accident that happened earlier that day. Michael settles himself down in the cot and strokes his hands on his teddy and falls asleep. He's had quite a day. His body is a little more prepared to react to the slightest worry, feeling or changes because today lots of chemicals related to stress filled his body and prepared him to survive a dangerous situation. They will remember this going forward and anything that feels similar, in terms of chemicals in the body or feelings in the nerves will alert going to the same kinds of reactions. It's almost like a soldier in training; he is learning that he *may* need to be on standby in the future.

However, his parents' actions helped him cope with the traumatic incident, and in time, Michael will be fine in terms of a healthy way to cope with stress. He will be able to 'self-regulate' because his parents have helped him regulate his feelings, and he is now learning to do this for himself. Due to the storytelling Michael's parents did with him, his upstairs house occupants made sense of this. The upstairs occupants chatted about this story from both sides of the house and put the story away in a memory box called 'minor car accident'. Michael could access this story whenever he wanted, and because it was talked about in the upstairs part of the house, it no longer sounded the sirens or silenced them very quickly. Although Michael was probably unaware of this memory box in terms of verbal language, it is one that he has tucked away. It is part of his life story now. His body remembers this feeling too.

References

Cozolino, L. (2006). *The neuroscience of human relationships: Attachment and the developing social brain* (2nd ed.). WW Norton & Co.

Le Doux, J. (2002). *The synaptic self. How our brains become who we are.* Penguin Books.

Le Doux, J. (2015). *Anxious. Using the brain to understand and treat fear and anxiety.* Viking.

Siegel, D. (2012). *The pocket guide to interpersonal neurobiology. An integrative handbook of the mind.* WW Norton & Co.

Siegel, D., & Bryson, T. (2012). *The whole brain child, 12 proven strategies to nurture your child's developing mind.* Robinson.

3 E-ttachment and the developing child

Introduction
How does this relate to the online world?

It is important for the reader to understand both attachment and trauma initially in relation to behaviours around the internet, gaming and relationships in cyberspace as I am talking about children and young people with these kinds of histories who are in the real world and who use the internet and cyberspace. In essence, you will learn about human behaviour both with or without electronics as a framework.

E-ttachment: why attachment patterns are changing in children and young people in relation to cyberspace

As you have seen, there are four types of attachment: secure and three types of insecure. Each attachment style has its own behaviours and characteristics. As we have seen, the attachment of a baby is created with the primary/main caregiver (usually the mother) and then close family members. In terms of the numbers of people in the babies/children's lives, there is an old saying of 'it takes a village to raise a child', and this will have been approximately 150 people known to the family. Furthermore, families tended to be close in both proximity, distance and closeness to each other and would often spend time with each other and their neighbours in the village.

However, this theory was originally posited in the last century, in the 1950s when families lived in/had what is called a 'nuclear family', that is Mum and Dad and an average of two children. Whist the theory is still relevant, I feel it could benefit from an update to include the changes of the technological age. Between the 1950s to late the 1980s, there were

DOI: 10.4324/9781003169390-4

usually one or two radios and televisions per family, and here's where technology begins to change the family attachment dynamics somewhat.

Technical progress

In the late 1970s and moving to the 1990s, some families would have owned VHS video players and home computers that played basic arcade-style games and could use a dot matrix printer (I haven't typed those words for a long time!), and children would gather around the new upcoming consoles to play games with each other on the TVs. Many sibling 'battles' have arguably commenced around these consoles in the 1980s and 1990s both on and off the consoles! Names like Sega and Nintendo began to appear as the new conversational norms of children and games like Mario or Sonic began to make their mark on children's gaming habits. Times on consoles tended to be restricted by the family TV needs (average families). If you were to speak to families during these times, it is more common to find the console in the main room rather than in a child's bedroom, although this is not to say it didn't happen that way.

Moving faster

Now fast-forward to 1996, the proposed dawn of the World Wide Web. Some families would have a few TVs and perhaps video players as well as some gaming consoles and perhaps a computer or two. Along comes the introduction of the internet connection on the family computer and suddenly the "village" becomes much bigger in terms of numbers of people that could be accessible via internet connections. Family divorce/separation rates are very different from those of the 1950s, 1960s and 1970s. Internet dial-up using a 'modem' is incredibly slow (and noisy).

Nearly now

Fast-forward again to 2007, and we are of an age during which families have computers and games consoles and are connected via fast-speed internet. Now marks the introduction of the smartphone and social media platforms begin to make their mark. Families are busy becoming involved in technology both in and out of home/work, and again the styles of family cohesion seem to be changing. The invention and competition of iOS and Windows operating systems become the new VHS/Betamax and the new HDD/Blu-Ray competition. Apple products win out when the iPod morphs into a computer in your pocket. Now a human can sit on their laurels and do in two minutes what it took me days to complete in the 1980s. They can have another human on their lap at their beck and call and touch in a matter of seconds. The world has indeed changed and now exists *out there and in here simultaneously*: where the in-here is now the biggest, ever-expanding village and universe we have ever encountered. Attachment just got an upgrade: *e-ttachment* is on the event horizon or perhaps already has hold.

Now and beyond

Over the last 30-plus years, I have partaken, watched and, more recently, researched the family dynamics in relation to technology, quantities and presence of devices within families, social media platforms, games consoles and the impact they have on families and my clients when discussing this in therapy. I feel attachment patterns are changing based on the innumerable presence and availability of technology to families and the sheer number of connections available to each person creating an exponential 'extended family and village'. Furthermore, I have watched how young children have appeared within my therapy room with varying degrees of cognitive and development changes and issues in line with the literature's 'expectations of child development'. These are both positive and negative, for which I suggest could be *partially* attributable and not causal to the use of devices. However, I am more likely to err on the side of early developmental attunement by parents, family members and others around the children and how brain architecture is formed through interpersonal relationships (Cozolino, 2006, 2014; Fonagy et al., 2004; Music, 2017; Schore, 2012; Siegel, 2012a, 2012b). Perhaps this is changing more so based on the presence, and of use, of technology and lowered levels of non-technology interactions.

There is no research that can 'prove' that technology causes delayed or cognitive impairment/development, as much of the research so far looks at issues that we cannot separate out from daily life. We are too complex for that, and our lives are multifactorial with and without technology. For example, terms like *screen time* are what academics call non-operational (which means we cannot measure accurately), and therefore, we are suggesting that interacting with devices is "linked to" certain issues. More on this later, however.

E-ttachment: how does it evolve, and what does it look like?

I along with some psychotherapists and cyber-psychology academics are very intrigued and fascinated by the presence of devices in babies' lives and how they understand these technologies. You only have to look at social media to see large volumes of videos of parents, siblings and others filming young children to see the interest, confusion and acceptance of these devices as a normal part of an interaction. The next time you see a baby/toddler video, take a look at how they look at the device. Does it look like this is a familiar object and one that is part of their world? Do they try to hold it, play with it and 'own it'? Do toddlers try to cover it up or push it out of the way like a baby sitting on their mothers' knee? Do they suddenly smile and light up as they are getting the attention, and is this because of the device or the parents' interest?

To be theoretical for a moment so you can see the overlap of technology into an infant's life and why I am proposing e-ttachment as a possible new or emerging process, there are stages of development I want to infer here. These are the early biological-imprinting circuitry, attachment processes and what our mind is and how it can be changed through intra- and interpersonal relationships. Understanding what and how our mind is and how it shaped by the world can offer us a way to support the development of a maturing brain in a world of technology. The mind is complex, and to date, there are many definitions, with one containing a cohort of approaches to how it is created emerges and is influenced by outside and inside forces (Siegel, 2016).

Using the theoretical propositions from earlier, I attempt to explain this so you can understand what e-ttachment is: biological-imprint circuity is about survival and how immediately after birth we innately connect with primary caregivers (in some animals, they follow the first "parent" they see). This, in turn, affects our attachment style, which, in turn, affects how we relate to ourselves and others and how we manage our emotional and self-regulation abilities and resources. I am suggesting the presence of digital technology that is almost always at hand and becomes part of this day-to-day interaction also affects our 'bonding' style and story that help us make sense of the world. It is different from other forms of technology as pre-smartphones, we often engaged with technology in smaller time constraints. The smartphone is metaphorically representing another person in this example, through its implied use of otherness and 'connections with others', not the physical device. To understand how and what I mean by this I teach the smartphone, tablet or device is *both a tool and a medium*. In this example, the medium is the relationship/mind/attachment influencer and perhaps the face I can see and touch.

This definition is neither positive nor negative in its assumptions as we do not know the full extent of the impact of an ever-present device; however, we do know that attachment patterns are affected by our emotional presence and right brain–to–right brain connections and actions. There is an implied negativity here, and it has been left open for debate as I think there is much more to be researched and understood, and only time will provide these answers. I am not demonising the smartphone or parents' ability to be present and attuned to babies and children, as I have already stated, the parenting role can be fraught with moments of misattunement without technology, and this has been occurring since parenting began. We are in an age in which fear and speculation are underpinning many of our approaches to technology, and perhaps, these are misguided and perhaps not.

2019/2020: e-ttachment, communication and social skills

At the end of 2020, it was suggested that there are approximately 4.9 billion people with access to the internet (Internet world stats, 2020). There are approximately 8 billion people in the world and counting. Now, in terms of evolutionary psychology, it is said that we can only hold four or five very special, or close, relationships in mind. Other people who surround us are said to be close family, friends, acquaintances and colleagues. In terms of literature, notably, the Dunbar effect suggests that we can only hold a certain number of relationships in our mind at any one time (Dunbar, 2009); this is often cited as 150 maximum. Logically, we can assume a village consisted of approximately 150 people. In 2020 and beyond, that village got a whole lot bigger, for both the parents and the child. This village could be as big as every internet connection around the world. Your 'cyber village' is therefore approximately 4.8 billion and counting (although not everyone is going to be contactable or be able to see you online, but you get my drift). *You may need a moment to let that sink in.*

Attachment is about how the parents relate to the child as well as the child to the parent. If we take the parent/carers use of technology, in this case, their number of connections on one social media platform, we might be talking about a village of 300-plus people. That's already double the amount we can hold in terms of brain development and evolution. However, the issue I want to add here is that's also 300-plus opinions on 'how to raise your baby', 'how to discipline', 'how to attach' and a good old-fashioned dose of parental peer pressure and socially desirable expectations from other users of those platforms, and that could be just for Mum. Imagine if Dad has 500-plus friends? Parenting is, as I have already said, a job with no manual or experts, yet one of the most common discussions I have in therapy with parents of young children is 'So

and So said on Facebook. . .' or 'In such and such parenting group/page/
speaker, they recommend this and that. . .'

In terms of how the parents/carers then build an attachment bond,
I suggesting that behaviours are changing in terms of the availability for
attunement, reflection, emotional presence and meeting the needs of
infants (not physical availability, e.g. having to work longer hours). However, given the fact that approximately 50% of the World population can,
on principle, access the internet, this seems relevant here as this number
will increase with the demonetisation of technology. Many poorer countries are also becoming smartphone-affluent, and where access was once
limited, the development of companies, such as those owned by Elon
Musk, that are putting satellites into orbit to provide continuous Wi-Fi
will only serve to increase this traffic, accessibility and presence of technology in a child's early life.

In turn, this creates a new interpersonal attachment system for babies,
children and young people. As a clinician, I am seeing much more of the
behaviours that reflect developmental trauma and attachment difficulties
(self-regulation skills). I am seeing some learning difficulties such as language acquisition and colloquialisms, non-verbal communication skills
and changing social skills of children in therapy. I am not attributing the
change in these presentations to the smartphone (as does a small number
of researchers claiming that poor mental health and unhappiness is due
to the rise of the iPhone), I suggest that changing parenting patterns and
communication of all humans are changing the way we "interrelate" as a species. The internet-ready technology has added a layer of complexity to
our way of being with each other and ourselves.

In doing so, this always connected–always disconnected dichotomy is
in the infancy of change, and we can neither say with accuracy this is
bad or good, helpful or not; however, it is currently changing. What we
know about how minds "work" is that when there are new, novel and
interesting stimuli, the mind is said to be **neuroplastic**, and this means
it begins to adapt, change and become familiar with the new until it
becomes normative. This is indeed a cyber-synaptic progression and one
that we can only be with. It isn't going away. Technology is our tool of
invention, creation, and like evolution, we have to see what the 'survival
of the fittest' is in terms of change and progress and who adapts best to
this.

Added to this are social behaviours that infants and children (before
1996) rarely had to contend with, such as being photographed/filmed
in almost every domain of their childhood lives for all and sundry. The
early-life album is public, documented and almost non-stop. Images are
often taken of developmental milestones, previously (pre-1996) kept as

personal mementos. Now, images of post-conception are uploaded and perused, mothers' wombs are on display too. Is anywhere in an infant's development sacred anymore?

Children pre-2007 didn't have to contend with the intermittent, constant or, at times, unrelenting sounds/actions from a device that 'steals' their parent's attention much more than a TV programme or book could? Having 300-plus people to attend to, via social media or games, is very time-consuming. This feeling is now in direct competition with babies' and children's needs in the here and now. It is rooted in attachment styles and 'self'-concepts. I wonder how infants/toddlers make sense of a thing (portable device) that is pointed at them, that is in so many interactions whilst the holder of 'the thing' coos, 'Smile'? Where is the device-free adoring face of the viewer, fascinated by every wrinkle and crinkle on your face?

Those micro-expressions that serve and return communication moments are being missed as the other person glances at the infant rather than being fully present. This leads infants and young children to encounter time and time again a feeling of missed attunement (feeling it in their bodies). Do they need to smile when they don't really feel like it? Babies' opinions, if we could only hear them, might be 'Why do I have to smile; why does that thing mean I have to smile? Why do you smile at me when you point it at me? And perhaps why do you only smile when that thing is pointed at me?' How utterly confusing.

Moreover, meaningful and deep eye contact may be missing in these moments due to devices blurring that direct visual of one face to another. There may be too quick an interaction (turning away from the tech to baby and back) for the baby to make any real sense of eye contact and facial cues. Smiles that are 'posed' for photographs (to encourage the photo smile) can feel very different to an authentic in the moment smile. Remember the neural expectation? We humans are very good at detecting the difference. I wonder whether the photo smile may become the one that babies begin to interpret as an everyday 'normal' smile if this becomes their baseline reference.

Added to this layered texture of attachment communication processes is a person's voice and how it 'sounds/feels' to the recipient. The intonation and prosody (tone) are how an infant makes sense of incoming messages with eyes and facial cues. If this happens to be very lovely sing-song voice whilst a 'thing' is pointed at them, they will feel perhaps that they are only special/wanted/needed when this 'thing' is present, and therefore, this becomes the focus of their attention and, in time, their attachment schema. If the 'thing' isn't present (i.e. in a pocket/out of sight), how will they learn to communicate without the 'thing' being present? This must be like an absent parent?

What about if the parent doesn't use the same voice/facial cues when the thing isn't present? Is this the new 'emotional regulator' of the parent? Are babies being momentarily connected to only for the parent/carer/relative to turn away and start smiling at the infant in the thing in their hands? Babies may even begin to feel despondent, angry or jealous of this 'thing' that steals their parents' attention; if they could speak would they be saying 'is the digital child in the device more important than me, the real thing out here?' And so, cue feelings of rejection, abandonment, confusion, hurt and perhaps more. If you think I'm being a little overdramatic, think back to time recently when you were taking to someone, only for them to take out their phone and text/reply/read/watch something in their hand that took the focus away from the conversation you were having. What did this really feel like? What did you tell yourself, and in doing this exercise, remember that you are an adult and have a thinking part of the brain that can rationalise about the other person's 'why'. If you really focus on the feeling, rather than the thoughts of how rude this other person was being, this is what an infant/young child experience. It's not a nice feeling!

Now, adding this to the attachment styles that we talked about in the early part of this book. If you're in the red or blue lanes and already have an insecure attachment style, what else gets added through repeated interactions and examples like this? Furthermore, to tie this back into the house analogy, for an infant, this is likely how they experience the missed attunement, for example the pathway messages to the house could be 'I'm feeling confused because I see a momentary (not genuine?) smiling face but hear a welcoming, connected and happy voice, but then they are looking at the digital child?' What do you think the house occupants make of this message? How do you make sense of this, especially when you don't have language to be able to rationalise, think or justify it? These can become part of their internal narrative and, rather like the stories I told earlier, embed the attachment style, or e-ttachment, more deeply.

To extend the preceding suggestions and bring this into the science even more so, an experiment conducted by Ed Tronick et al. (1978) highlights just how distressing misattunement for a child is; in fact, videos updated and widely available on YouTube show that the young child in the experiment loses her muscle control and becomes highly dysregulated. If this becomes a norm in an infant's world, then we could have a generation of misattuned children who will struggle with interpersonal relationships and skills. Or maybe this has already occurred?

For reflections around this topic, have a listen to Joanna Fortune and Jocelyn Brewer on *Cyber Synapse* podcast episodes with me. I'm suggesting that 'attachment' is changing very surreptitiously rather speedily and incrementally. At this stage, we do not have enough evidence to say it is technology, and I suppose I am rather like some cyber-psychology authors making assumptions and observations in order to provide the reader with my thinking around e-ttachment whilst the evidence is perhaps barely there? Could I be worrying unnecessarily? Perhaps, however, I have noticed how difficult it can be for people (younger than 30 and increasingly getting to the older generation who did not grow up with this technology) to stay present in therapy for the full 50 minutes and without at some point referencing their social media lives or taking their phone or smartwatch out to look. I wonder, as a therapist, if this tolerance level will decrease over the years and if it will be attributed to this theory here. More robust research is needed, please!

Yet this is going to be an interesting and perhaps difficult area to research, due to the fact that there are so many other variables that are confounding (haver an impact) such as parents' ability to be fully present and show up, their attachment histories and difficulties and the possession of the knowledge of the 'world's best parent' (I've only ever seen these in Disney movies by the way or seen them posted on social media by the parents themselves). There are going to be variables on babies' temperaments and brain development, notwithstanding the impediments of individual differences, the number of children per household, socioeconomics and whether parents want to/need to work, how educated they are, how closely they have other supportive figures in their lives and so on. Research in this area can really only ever be correlational, and this means to suggest that we can say it is linked to, but we can never say causes.

Returning to attachment processes, communication and brain development in children, clinicians and researchers really highlight eye contact and non-verbal communication as the serve-and-return right brain–to–right brain interactions between parent and child which underpin attachment processes and resilient brain development. I suggest that these contingent moments of connection are changing surreptitiously. In terms of quantity and quality of those moments, I believe we are moving away from the child being the focus of attention to a distracted parent not necessarily distracted by a device alone but by the amount of sheer information they must contain within their minds at any one time in today's society and exacerbated by 'cyber'-based products that enhance the peer pressure and size of the village one must attend to. We are now consuming as much information per day as a person in the 1400s would consume in a lifetime (Kwik, 2020). Consuming this information, which is so plentiful, may feel like trying to drink water out of a pressurised hose.

This information nowadays doesn't necessarily always arrive from digital devices either. We live in an age in which we have lots of child-related practitioners who become involved in children's lives in many ways, and each one of them has read, learned and shared their own knowledge, alongside all those social media posts they have been influenced by too. Even with or without a university undergraduate degree, everyone is now an expert on a/the topic, and this filters into the life of each baby who is born in this digital age. It feels like information overload, and the children are bearing the brunt of our overflowing tanks of 'know-it-all-isms'.

The influence on growing up in the digital age

As children begin to communicate with each other in settings like nursery and school, they learn the précis of social behaviours and in-group/out-group processes. Their language skills are developed, and communication with others is increased. They learn socially desirable and undesirable behaviours and begin to learn about group cohesion and friendships. They learn to take turns and share (age- and stage-appropriate), and they learn how to handle, manage and regulate their emotions as they reach stages of conflict, envy, frustration and many more emotional encounters. A good skill set for a young person consist of social *and* emotional intelligence, and this will include self-regulation and empathy for others. However, if the early experience of the child has been with a parent who did not help them learn to self-regulate, correct language pronunciation, spend quality time with them and help them develop their skills they will begin to learn them elsewhere. If this means through a device and/or the device is used as a babysitter/pacifier, then the skill sets of young children are likely going to be influenced by these interactions rather than those of face-to-face contact with a corporeal 'other'.

However, when you look at the examples of what has already happened in history, we might be looking at a scaremongering issue here, that unless children get 100% contact from parents that they won't develop "normally". I'd like to introduce you to the hyperbole surrounding TV, magazines, video games and, now, devices. Also, a great book on these kinds of moral panics is a book called *Moral Combat* (Markey & Ferguson, 2017). What we do know is that *some* children are affected in this way, and most are not. Most children do not become sociopaths, violent or illiterate because they have a digital device in close proximity and/or use. We just do not have enough evidence yet to warrant many of these claims, and we do not have enough evidence to say that children are losing the ability to do or behave certain ways, nor are these devices solely responsible for issues such as mental health, crime and reports of increasing depression in young people (more on this later).

To be clear, I am suggesting the way children become attached to another human being and learn to self-regulate, and this includes how the brain architecture is formed and maintained, is changing. I am neither saying this is for good or bad. I think it is different and requires us to look at the purpose of attachment, which in its most basic form is to survive and to learn *how to socialise in a group*. In terms of passive TV/ video games research, we know that in today's society, the device connects us to other people, lots of other people, so perhaps the brain and attachment patterns are adapting to accommodate *more social relationships and more connections?* Perhaps this is too much in terms of mind-based capabilities? For example the potential to be connected to 8 billion people scares, fascinates and concerns me; however, unlike a newborn, I'm not at the beginning of my life not knowing any other way. I have other information within my history of learning that includes a small village of people, and now I possess the knowledge and experience of increasing connections. This is perhaps why I find this difficult to think about. I have a *before and after the Internet* and can compare these experiences.

If this increase in 'village' is indeed the case and the sheer numbers of people we have to hold in mind increases, then I feel quite confident in saying that brains are currently changing to adapt to this. We call this adaptability and change **neuroplasticity**, and I am proposing that this is happening to all people who are currently users of this technology. Therefore, children and young people are developing a skill of needing to maintain many of these relationships and in doing so are becoming *more invested in numerous relationships*, and perhaps this dilutes their potency rather than the quoted opposite of less connectedness. I suspect this could bring about an increase in the kinds of anxious attachment behaviours and feelings proposed in the original attachment theory as we may be in a better position to understand how children feel when confronted with a larger or increasing number of connections (adults too).

I suspect this may be the behaviour change we actually see in children, young people and adults who are in the process of trying to work out where they need to connect or disconnect with others online, maintain, ignore and/or walk away from certain interactions and posts. It's a tricky situation for all of us when the *medium of connection* to others is also the *tool* for our work/school/pleasure. How do we separate and make distinctions between our own space and time when it can be intruded on, invaded or taken away from us at any moment (by parents, internet-connectivity issues, the government, etc.?) This could be enough to create anxiety feelings just reading this.

Furthermore, when teaching, I tend to ask people what their attachment style is. I then ask them if this relates to/through their device. Are they ambivalent about the apps they use or the people they speak to through these apps? Are they avoidant of them, and does it bring them feelings of unease? Mostly what I see is a narrative of varying attachment styles through the day for varying numbers of reasons, and this also reflects the sheer number of connections we now have as having a direct impact on the numbers of attachments we have. Now for just a moment, imagine you are a high school child who has been asked to do some research online for homework; invariably, they will switch to having, or already have, social media on in the background. Now imagine that on this day there had been an event at school with a peer. Would they avoid social media whilst attempting to do their homework, or would they look to see what is being gossiped about? I'm sure I never had this when researching through a book and was able to concentrate on my homework (not that I always enjoyed it), and sometimes, I used to stop doing homework if there was a TV programme I wanted to watch (or fibbed and said I had completed it). This is now an exacerbated distraction with the invention of YouTube. For some children, they may begin to get activities (homework) muddled up with social situations (social media apps), and this will influence both learning and e-ttachment.

Levels of secure attachment and vulnerabilities

The estimated level of secure attachment styles is 59%; however, the research is perhaps dated in this realm due to the questions and surveys now asked of the general population are generally aimed at the living arrangements, income status and so on. I wonder how secure and safe some of the children in the UK feel in 2020 and beyond. There are also many single-parent/distanced/divorced/separated families, children in kinship families, the 'system' of looked-after children, refugees, immigrants, NEET (not in education, employment or training) and those who do not have a 'category'. Current figures estimate that the number of single/lone-parent families in the UK lies in the region of 2.9 million (Office for National Statistics, 2019), which is approximately 15% of the population. Figures that look at children in the UK who are in the 'looked after' sector, what is often referred to as the 'system', is currently 80,000 (UK Government, 2020), which looks like a low percentage; however, some of the categories listed earlier do not get included in this figure, and if children live with relatives, they are often omitted from these figures also.

Why is this section about children who are perhaps not living with their original families even necessary? I'm sure you have seen on the news, reports, media and probably under the policies in government, vulnerable children are often referred to as needing our help. How would you identify a vulnerable person or child, and how does this apply to the online/digital world? First, let me say that *all* children are vulnerable by the very fact they are children or young people.

Second, when online, ***everyone is vulnerable***. This is worth remembering for adults too. Third, and most important, when speaking to vulnerability or resilience of children in the online space, this is about the skill sets and resources they have or do not have, not what makes them more likely to be open to any form of abuse, which again covers *all children*. Fourth, vulnerability is a complex definition (in the UK) referring to children who are, in general, in the looked-after system, criminal justice system, those with learning or special needs, mental health diagnoses and socio-economic status that classify them as living in poverty, included in immigration or detention, involved in gangs, and/or out of mainstream education, and this is not exhaustive of all the characteristics of this definition (Children's Commissioner England, 2019). In fact, we are all vulnerable to a degree to anyone deciding to attack or manipulate us in any way, shape or form (on or offline). Allow me to suggest that *vulnerability is both a noun and a verb*. It is something we *are* and something we *do*.

I am suggesting that it is by our very nature of using online technology that makes us vulnerable, not a flaw in our genetics, personality traits or characteristics so often reported by media and academics. ***Vulnerability is a proposition I am making that it is both a verb *and* a noun***, (though this sentence will likely enrage English Teachers as vulnerability is not a verb), and once this is understood, we can perhaps look at human errors in the virtual, digital and cyber realms in a different light (Knibbs, 2019a, 2019b).

How and why this is important in terms of online behaviours

I am highlighting that trauma and attachment are far more of a significant factor in online behaviours than socially deemed levels of vulnerability based on socio-economic factors, living accommodations and mental health diagnoses alone. This is due to the impact on and the development of brain function, architecture, cognitive processing, social skills, emotional regulation and all the other issues, whereby attachment/trauma (environmental or relational) impacts a child ability to think clearly, reason and take managed and appropriate risks. It is the impact of these issues that affects a child's behaviour in the corporeal world and subsequently the online/digital space more so than any other, and the more trauma/attachment difficulties the more we could use the word vulnerable. This is child (human) development and an intra- and interpersonal relationships issue more than family/socio-economic status alone. There are many children who live with the 'nuclear family' set-up who have encountered attachment/trauma events, and these are often omitted from the research into vulnerable children as, on the surface, they don't 'look' vulnerable by virtue of the fact they have a two-parent family. Yet they make up a large amount of my therapeutic work for the cyber-based issues. What do we miss when we omit this factor? Who is to say that a securely attached child won't be manipulated, attacked or hacked in cyberspace? And might this just be due to a lack of 'cyber–street smart skills'?

References

Children's Commissioner England. (2019). *Childhood vulnerability in England*. www.childrenscommissioner.gov.uk/report/childhood-vulnerability-in-england-2019/

Cozolino, L. (2006). *The neuroscience of human relationships: Attachment and the developing social brain* (1st ed.). WW Norton & Co.

Cozolino, L. (2014). *The neuroscience of human relationships: Attachment and the developing social brain* (2nd ed.). WW Norton & Co.

Dunbar, R. (2009). The social brain hypothesis and its implications for social evolution. *Annals of Human Biology*, *36*(5), 562–572. https://Doi.org/10.1080/03014460902960289

Fonagy, P., Gergely, G., Jurist, E., & Target, M. (2004). *Affect regulation, mentalization and the development of the self*. Karnac.

Knibbs, C. (2019a). *Risk, danger or cybertrauma? Cyberspace and the impact on CYP and the therapist*. BACP CYP Conference. London.

Knibbs, C. (2019b). www.childrenandtech.co.uk

Kwik, J. (2020). *Limitless. Upgrade your brain, learn anything faster and unlock your exceptional life*. Hay House.

Markey, P., & Ferguson, C. (2017). *Moral combat. Why the war on violent video games is wrong*. BenBella Books.

Miniwatts Marketing Group. Internet World Stats. (2020). https://internetworldstats.com/stats.htm

Music, G. (2017). *Nurturing natures. Attachment and children's emotional, sociocultural and brain development* (2nd ed.). Routledge.

Office for National Statistics. (2019). www.ons.gov.uk/peoplepopulationandcommunity/birthsdeathsandmarriages/families/bulletins/familiesandhouseholds/2019

Schore, A. (2012). *The science of the art of psychotherapy*. WW Norton & Co.

Siegel, D. (2012a). *The developing mind. How relationships and the brain interact to shape who we are.* WW Norton & Co.

Siegel, D. (2012b). *The pocket guide to interpersonal neurobiology. An integrative handbook of the mind.* WW Norton & Co.

Siegel, D. (2016). *Mind. A journey to the heart of being human.* WW Norton & Co.

Tronick, E., ALs, H., Adamson, L., Wise, S., & Brazelton, B. (1978). The infant's response to entrapment between contradictory messages in face-to-face interaction. *Journal of the American Academy of Child Psychiatry, 17,* 1–13. https://doi.org/10.1016/S0002-7138(09)62273-1

United Kingdom Government. (2020). *National statistics.* https://explore-education-statistics.service.gov.uk/find-statistics/children-looked-after-in-england-including-adoptions/2020

4 The neurobiology of online behaviour

A new proposition

Introduction
Attachment and trauma in online behaviours

In short, any child who has an insecure attachment issue or style will seek to do a number of things to help calm or soothe themselves, with a primary focus of regulating how they feel on a moment-by-moment basis. These coping strategies may not seem logical to you. When they occur in the online world, this may seem even less so. Within this chapter, it is highly unlikely that the focus is on securely attached children; however, please think that the following can apply to any child you have, live with, know or work with. Let's focus on how insecure attachment issues often present in the real world and then double-click on them for how they often present in the online world. These children will look to reaffirm that they don't belong (to the family/surroundings or online spaces) by the following:

1 Creating situations in which they are rejected/punished therefore affirming their feelings. They feel are somehow bad or to blame (shame). This is a destructive pattern that often tires out those who are doing their best to help the child or young person. In therapy, I often hear the adults 'complain' of the bad behaviour, the outbursts, the broken furniture, the swearing and so on and how they, the adult, cannot cope anymore or are fed up and at times on the verge of fighting back with violence or destructive language. This really is difficult for all, and it can feel relentless. In terms of what this behaviour will look like online, they may irritate/become destructive or 'flame' (wind up) others (deliberately or otherwise); they will join groups in which they can be bullies or bullied; they will engage in gaming behaviours that mirror this also. They may cyber-self-harm in the form of self-**cyberbullying**/trolling (they bully themselves

DOI: 10.4324/9781003169390-5

and make it appear as though it is others). They may create a situation whereby you remove/ban the device/console.

2   Behaving like they don't want you to leave and want you to be included in all they do and you do. This can feel clingy/overbearing to you the adult. In therapy, I often hear that the adult cannot get space and time to themselves and that this is tiring. It's like the toddler stage in which the child wants to be with you even when you visit the toilet! It can mean that the adult seemingly doesn't get any adult and non-parenting time. This is another very difficult time for all. Regarding online behaviour, they may always have a drama that needs your help; for example the console doesn't work properly, or they need your help for homework (that you feel they are completely capable of). They may watch things that you feel are inappropriate so you spend time overseeing what they are doing (it feels like you cannot trust them).

3   Running away. This can leave them frightened, and you are beside yourself and often feeling like a failure. I hear in therapy that this leaves the adults feeling like they are doing the caring 'wrong' and leads to a lot of self-blame or 'other blame', whereby the child is labelled as naughty and not giving a hoot. This is a very difficult time as this is often fraught with safety concerns for the child or young person. In terms of online behaviour, they may arrange to meet someone in real life to assist with their running away. They may also engage in games/activities that metaphorically whisk them away (psychologically), and they may visit websites that are scary/inappropriate and leave their history open so you can see that they have visited these sites, as this can create anxiety/distress for you.

4   Dissociating or non-responsive. This can be draining on those around the child. Often in therapy, I hear the adults say that the child is unresponsive, ignorant, daydreams and will/does not partake in the family dynamics. This can be a difficult situation as the efforts to include the child or young person can feel like they are unheard or should not be bothered. This can leave adults feeling like they have nothing more to offer and can/do give up trying. In terms of online behaviour, this is a little like running away; however, they may binge-watch TV shows or YouTube videos and have no recollection of what they watched or time spent doing so. They may find themselves watching scary/graphic or traumatic videos in order to see just how far they can push themselves in terms of 'managing emotions' (e.g. hiding behind their hands). They may become so absorbed in games/ devices that you cannot gain any attention or have a conversation.

They may also 'rage out' when you try to engage with them as they engage in the dissociative online behaviour.

5   Have suicidal feelings, thoughts or even behaviours. This is a very difficult set of behaviours as this is the most concerning issue in therapy for the adults when they feel like they are 'on edge' constantly and worrying about the child's thoughts/behaviours and intentions and fear of reprise should they miss anything. For the children, it can be felt/seen to be smothering as they often report that the questions 'Are you okay?' and 'Are you sure?' are asked excessively and feel intrusive. In terms of online behaviour, they may visit sites that discuss suicide or varying forms of self-harm and mutilation, and they may spend time watching or listening to songs/videos on YouTube with a focus on these issues. They may begin to spend more time on these sites and withdraw from social activities or even the family. However, they may conversely exhibit none of these activities and things may look as they always have done for this child.

6   Self-harm in varying forms such as substance use/misuse, eating disorders, sexual behaviours and/or self-injurious behaviours. This is also a difficult situation as often the adults will try to remove the behaviour/substance/device, and this can create situations of anger/distress and escalation. This can feel like the child is in self-destruct mode, and the adults often report that they feel/are powerless. This may be the same for the child or young person. In terms of online behaviours, they may become regular users of sites that discuss or hint at self-harming behaviours and ways to engage in this, they may use social media sites where this behaviour is discussed and there may be code words around these issues. (Social media sites often remove [*some] posts/images relating to self-harm). As before, they may engage in cyber self-harm. Furthermore, the form of sexual self-harm behaviours can result in further issues such as grooming/exploitation. (See my training, or next book for more information on this as it is too large a topic to add here.)

Most of these behaviours are the result of shame and, or fear of abandonment, now or in the future. Each child will display their preferred default response in order to manage the distressing feelings. However, this is not normally a conscious choice (most of the time), so asking the child to explain may be incomprehensible for them to justify. In general, they won't know their why, and this can further compound shame.

To illustrate this, I ask if you can come up with a rational explanation for why many human beings fear public speaking? This is actually one of the biggest fears for most people, and when we look at it rationally, there isn't an overly demanding biology-based reason for the fear. There's no tiger on stage, no bear at the front of the class (not a real one anyway).

It is actually a social reason. It's about fear of humiliation, shame, ridicule, rejection and, most of all, failure, and do these seem rational to you? All these things are about feelings. These are not life-threatening; they are our reasons for not wanting to make a fool of ourselves in front of others. Where do you think this fear originates, childhood at a guess? So, if you have a fear of public speaking, what steps do you take to avoid it, conquer it, work with it and so on? Are they rational, do you even know you are doing it at the time?

As you can see, attachment issues are not always logical to the outsider you have to get behind the behaviour to communication and the reason. It may not make sense to you at first glance; then again does the fear of holes, a fear of balloons, a fear of spiders, lions, tigers and bears, oh my?

As children (and sometimes in adulthood) we try to avoid being hurt at all costs. This is often the primary underlying reason for these insecure attachment behaviour communications. And so we need to listen carefully, compassionately and empathetically as the adults in their world.

Polyvagal theory and the online world

Before we begin looking at behaviours in relation to cyberspace that tie together attachment and trauma and our basic biological behaviours and functions in the world, I need to briefly explain a theory that underpins my thinking in this area called the **polyvagal theory** (Porges, 2011). A little confession, however. I have been introducing this theory to you already within the stories about the brain and the body and trauma. As I progress, the theory may begin to make much more sense for you, and you may find yourself getting excited about all this new 'stuff' that helps us understand the world in a much more complex way.

Let's start with biology 101. The human body is made up of trillions of cells that have one function in life, and this is to survive. These look like very simple choices of move from or towards a stimulus, for example away from danger and towards food. The body also does this with feelings and perceptions of threat and safety. When we notice a threat of any sort, we can say this is a stressor, and this is a word you are likely familiar with in terms of 'stress'.

Our bodies and brain generally opt for a retreat-and-rest response (when possible) when under distress and to go/grow when under eustress (good stress). This constant monitoring is managed primarily by your nervous system 24/7/365 without you telling it to do so. This system is called the autonomic nervous system, and it is through these pathways called the vagus nerve that information is carried to and from the brain. Remember our messengers in the story who run up and down the pathways? Those pathways are the nervous system, and the messengers are the transmissions of energy and information along these pathways.

It turns out our bodies keep track of how safe (real or perceived) or under stress we are, or feel we are, all the time, and much of this happens out of our awareness. Imagine if our brain had to decipher and pay attention to and think about every single message it received, every single moment of the day; that would be exhausting. So the brain has learned to pay attention to signals that reach a certain threshold; for example if the heart beats regularly, the brain recognises this as an activity it can pay less attention to; however, if there was a message that there was a sharp pain or faster beats around the heart, this would carry a louder/faster message which the brain would pay immediate attention to.

Remember how Amy R is posed to listen to the messages as familiar or unfamiliar and to press the alarm buttons for unfamiliar and unsure? This is an example of how she decides based on everyday regular familiar and the 'out of the ordinary'. In everyday speak, those moments can be summed up as "What the heck was that?"

This nervous system 'monitoring' is what Stephen Porges (2011) named **neuroception** (i.e. nervous system threat detection), and it tracks for example our heart rate, breathing and how they are synchronised to each other, our internal organs and how we feel when we are in the company of others. When we feel appropriately safe, it lets us know we are okay to communicate with others around us rather than detecting by listening or looking out for the tiger in the bush. We can concentrate on being here in the now.

We see this when we look at humans who are sitting (or standing) with each other, looking comfortable in their surroundings, chatting and smiling in a coherent manner and nicely regulated (balanced). This is the 'green lane' that I introduced you to earlier. It feels nice to be here, and people often talk about feeling like they are in the present when they are here.

When we are under threat, stress, distressed or 'emotionally dysregulated', in some way the branches of the systems are concerned with either "speed up" (the red lane) and mobilisation towards safety, that is get away or 'slow down' (the blue lane), which includes shutting down completely, fainting or feigning death for survival. This threat is not decided by whether something is considered a 'big deal' by outsiders or is a life threat; it only needs to feel like that. The sensitivity of the nervous system of the person experiencing the threat is what matters, and some are more sensitive than others. There is a plant called the sensitive/nervous plant (mimosa), and if you gently touch the edge of the leaf, the whole plant retreats and curls up.

And there's more; our eyes are connected to the highest branch of the vagal nerve and thanks to Andrew Huberman's work in the public domain (2020), I can tell you with a huge wow factor that your eyes are indeed a part of your brain that sits outside the skull. Porges (2011), talks about the muscles surrounding the eyes, called the orbicularis oculi, and how they are controlled by our social engagement communication systems (the green safe and social lane). We have what he calls a 'neural expectancy' which I explained earlier. For example, when I smile at you, my face muscles crinkle the skin, and you see this and interpret whether this is genuine or a threat. I am likely to expect a returned smile or form of communication that meets my smiling at you. If you return a facial expression that does not meet my expectation, for example you grimace or turn your nose up, I am likely to feel discord, and this results in a feeling of discomfort or stress.

When the nervous system becomes highly activated the communication pathways often get overridden. Therefore, when we are experiencing a big dose of stress, for example fear, shame, anger and the like, we can't speak or listen accurately. Our pupils increase in size to take in maximum information or they focus on the immediate threat. Our hearing is focused on lower frequency sounds, and of course, we are likely to be heading out of the green lane and into the red or blue. Survival is biologically driven, and we don't actively or consciously get to choose what our brain and body does in these situations.

To recap from the stories, where you read about the three paths – green, red and blue – that lead to the house I have been talking about the autonomic nervous system and how this information is brought to the house to be deciphered like the signals from your body that travel to the brain through the front door of the house. What occurs in our body is rather like the order of messengers arriving at the house and depends on the severity of the danger and whether they are walking or running. Where the stress is low the top pathway messenger arrives, and we speak or perhaps use our facial muscles to convey how we are feeling. If our communication isn't working, we may feel more stress, and the first messenger is beaten to the door by the 'speed up' messenger so we can run away or fight the danger. (Think walking off in a huff or shouting.) When all else fails the 'slow down' system is as fast as 'The Flash' and tramples all over the other two messengers and pushes their way through the front door (think catatonic responses or fainting).

The false safety zone of digital communication and interactions

Why am I writing about stress, biology and attachment in relation to cyberspace? The polyvagal theory is a way for us to understand how human beings feel safe in the world and have evolved in terms of connection and communication. However, what is important here is when and how our communication system feels like there is no immediate threat or danger and how it can be 'tricked' into a false safety when engaging with or through a device. We often are in safe spaces when we use our devices such as the home, in our lounges or when out in public when we have done a quick scan of our environment and deemed it to be safe and so we feel safe as we pick up or open our device. It's a trusted 'other', and there is no tangible warning signal from the digital space for our nervous systems to decode in transit, our shields are down and we are (mostly) unaware of it. This suggests why we can be so quick to react to those stress responses through our devices, and this forms the foundation of **cybertrauma** and its impact (see my website www.childrenandtech. co.uk for the definition of this issue).

In the stories earlier, I talked about babies and how they get a non-verbal imprinted message about safety 'in the real world', and this becomes a superfast signal that our bodies and brains implicitly trust without question. This signal is conveyed at a particular distance and that is the eye gaze distance of approximately 30 to 40 cm (when measuring during breastfeeding). If we add in the sense of touch here, you can see how this distance is paired with safety and the movement of our digits on the digital screen or keyboard. So here you are gazing at your iPhone, tablet, laptop or computer screen, touching, stroking (scrolling) the screen or keys. Have you ever guessed how close on average you are to it? Can you take an educated guess now? Well opticians/ophthalmologists have proposed this distance is approximately, wait for it . . . 30 to 60 cm on average (Rosenfield, 2011).

You're not surprised by this fact now, are you? Could I have been unconsciously layering information to you one idea over another? I do hope so and yet this ride isn't finished. Notwithstanding these facts as being enough to wow you, for just a moment, think about when you are gazing into the eyes of a person you love. Have you ever noticed you are proximally quite close to them? (Probably a similar distance.) And here's one of the biological things that happens at this distance (no, not that). You get a burst of a neurochemical called oxytocin which is known as a social bonding/trust hormone, especially where touch is involved (Field, 2014). So, when you are feeling safe, your eyes are focused on something in close proximity, your body and brain sense the familiarity of this distance. If you had a good enough experience as a baby, this distance feels safe/trustworthy by default. This is your intimate zone of proximal safety, and when you are in this zone, you get a familiar dose of neurochemicals, associated behaviours and feelings.

If for any reason you felt stressed, bored, lonely, isolated, sad, happy and/or more, you are likely to try to reach out to someone to communicate this and have your need of touch, being seen or being heard met by that other. If no one is there physically, you might do this through the screen. And herein lies the strongest motivator of human behaviour and device use. It's called attachment, bonding, socialising and, of course, is a biological drive that's satisfied by the very distance of your eyes and screen where *the other person* is housed and you can virtually touch and caress them, so imagine what virtual reality may help us do! You can see this in toddlers who walk towards a TV and stand at this distance to the screen (given the chance). Yes, there is also a spike of dopamine (and other neurochemicals) as you are witnessed and validated. This is the argument currently used in the mainstream media to describe **addiction** to socialising. I talk more about the ideas of virtual reality, addiction and young people later.

I am suggesting that as we sit with our devices in our hands or in front of our eyes in this way our bodies and brains are 'fooled' into what I call the *false safety zone of digital communication* that we are now about to enter. Once we do enter, we can become absorbed, immersed and involved into the activities much like we would in a face-to-face situation. Many of the activities we engage with through our devices are social, emotional and psychological (unless we are doing something pragmatic like online banking, spreadsheets or other 'working'-style tasks). The biology cues we feel are that this is a safe space to be in, and our social engagement system reads the cues as such. Our bodies are now open to a plethora of hijacks without neuroceptive warnings because devices do not emit the same level of corporeal cues as a person sitting or standing close to us.

Now this might sound scary; however, most days and most of our interactions in cyberspace do not result in the circumnavigation of this system, and we often have a good experience in the cyber/digital realm. Yet the reason we can become so heightened by online behaviours is because we are now in polarity with our neuronal expectations of what should happen in these circumstances; that is our brains have a set of expectations based on everyday behaviours in the land of 'normal' communications patterns that we are used to. Remember the section on babies learning to communicate, reciprocity and how the dyad of conversation is the serve and return pattern? The digital space is now changing this pattern, and we are becoming confused and enraged by this sabotage, which for some of us happens multiple times per day.

Let's take the eyes for just one second and think about the suggestion that we gaze, (perhaps adoringly) into our technology. This makes an assumption that we are biologically primed to feel safe and social, as we approach our technology before we type our password in, click the mouse and so on. This will produce a priming effect for an expectation that we will be in a dialogue with A. N. Other, even though we accept this could likely be **asynchronous** (delayed and take time). This is not a new form of communication for many of us adults as we have been doing this through the form of writing letters and emails for some time. We are getting used to two speeds/forms of communication with other humans, and since the advent of social media, this is increasing the way we now communicate in a delayed manner, and we are seemingly able to manage this. More on this later, when we can be seen to not manage this.

Second, the mainstream media would have you believe that young people cannot do this at all and have an expectation to be in synchronous, immediate conversations at all times, citing 'delayed gratification' as the source of their discontent. I mean, if we bring our children into the world and teach their biology, as infants, that we are there to communicate with them, how dare we say they are broken in some way for having this very expectation hardwired? I do not find this with the young people I work with, and we often discuss their desire to slow things down, have some respite and not be at the beck and call of others (with their 'presence' being seen by others through various and numerous devices/platforms).

Or are we actually saying that young people are frustrated and impatient because we created some of these feelings in their early infancy by being busy, overworked or distracted ourselves? Perhaps the way we communicate with children has changed over the last 25 years, and we are now seeing the results of a generation in which blame is attributed to young people, yet we the adults created this very situation? I know that kind of stings a bit, doesn't it?

That feels like a momentous paragraph, and of course, it is. Yet we have a great opportunity here when we share robust research and evidence-based findings and understand human behaviour deeply rather than scratching the surface, pathologising or scare-mongering parents into believing their children have issues that cannot be 'fixed' and indeed may be 'their fault', which, of course, you may have believed through my rhetorical question.

References

Field, T. (2014). *Touch* (2nd ed.). MIT Press.

Friedman, L. (Host) (2020, November 16). *Lex Friedman podcast. Andrew Huberman: Neuroscience of optimal performance* [Video Podcast]. www.youtube.com/watch?v=K tj050DxG7Q&list=PLrAXtmErZgOdP_8GztsuKi9nrraNbKKp4

Porges, S. (2011). *The polyvagal theory. Neurophysiological foundations of emotions, attachment, communication and self-regulation.* WW Norton & Co.

Rosenfield, M. (2011). Computer vision syndrome. A review of ocular causes and potential treatments. *Ophthalmic Physiological Optics, 31*(5), 502–515. https://doi.org/ 10.1111/j.1475-1313.2011.00834.x

5 Biology before brain

Why states precede
disinhibition online

Introduction
Using devices is all attachment and relationship processes then?

Let's take a step back and go back to the eyes and what happens biologically with and through them (to add more complexity). It has become
apparent that when we focus on things in our environment, we have
several responses that also occur in the area known as the brain. These are
also tied into the stress–response systems. So let's travel back in time to
when we could hunt or be hunted.

If you think about cats and consider what they do when they hunt you
will notice that they have a few striking behaviours. First, when hunt-
ing, they try their very best not to be noticed by the prey. They do this
through slow movements in their bodies and tracking with their eyes
whilst remaining still, watching and waiting before leaping to strike. So
let's focus on the eyes and what's happening for the cat as it is tracking the
prey. As the predator's pupils focus on the prey, they momentarily dilate
to enhance the amount of light and information coming into the eyes and
brain to quickly work out the likely trajectory and intended moves of the
prey. The head of the cat is very still, and the eyes move in their sockets to
'dial in' on the prey. The prey may also remain still if it 'detects' the predator (neuroception in action!). In this moment, stillness and vision become
the priority for both predator and prey. The eyes become the mechanism
by which the victory of life and death can be won. The stress response in
this case will be a run for your life or a run to catch your meal.

Now consider a human in the bushes (or down a dark alley); they
hear a rustling sound close to them, and their nervous system asks, "Am
I predator or prey?" The stress response dilates the pupils and enhances
the ability hear, and the eyes dart about looking to see what the sound is
connected to. If they can only see a small aspect of the unknown object,
for example (i.e. it's camouflaged or seems small or unfamiliar such as

DOI: 10.4324/9781003169390-6

shiny like a knife), the eyes limit the amount of peripheral information they pay attention to and, with laser-like precision, focus on the object in what is called convergent vision. Therefore, weapons are often focused on during an attack and not the face of the assailant or location.

If this object happens to be a small screen, such as a smartphone in our hands, and our eyes are focusing, through this convergent vision process, the same biological pathways are likely to be triggered in terms of the stress response. Our brains initially react to what our biology is doing, and then our thinking occurs in relation to the event. Our brain will be trying to decipher and process the biology and whether we are converging our vision for a threat detection or whether we are dialling in for safety and social reasons. We could be confusing our biology and creating a repetition of a well-rehearsed attachment process that is unsafe, rather than feeling safe as I suggested earlier. It will all be dependent on the person's default past experiences and what the biology 'speaks to' when the eyes converge or are triggered by the proximal 30-cm distancing.

Moreover, the physiological and emotional state prior to picking up a device will have an impact on the stress response and can impact what we do and how we feel when we enter into this virtual space looking for a need to be met. For example, a client in therapy told me about the anger she felt at finding out her partner had cheated on her. Whilst her partner was in the process of packing her bags, she picked up her partner's phone (feeling angry and betrayed) and began to delete messages, pictures and contacts in the hope she could 'delete' the event and people involved. My client's socialising system was certainly set to 'seek and destroy', and her convergent vision will have heightened her focus when using the device. She told me that for weeks she hated her phone. I suggest here that her biology had associated the feelings of anger and betrayal with the convergent vision and the distancing of the device and that she had looked at it often hoping to have her needs met of removing the discomfort and pain. The phone was not to blame, per se; however, her feelings were associated with the device. I am sure we all have an experience of this when we need to do 'work' on our computer and can feel like this. I suspect this has become exacerbated during the lockdowns for many of us.

What about other things we do in, on and through our devices?

Herein lies another layered complication that because our device allows us to engage in 'cognitive'-based tasks as well as socialising (e.g. spreadsheets, calculator or books vs videoconferencing), we cannot distinguish between these processes separately enough to measure them accurately as many suggest. Cognitive processes such as reading require us to think about what we are doing and can be evocative, provocative or emotive. Take for example what you have been doing so far, as I have asked you to recall memories, consider other events and possibilities and, of course, naturally your mind will wander to you thinking about your life, situation or that of others you know as you focus on the words with convergent vision. This convergent vision is what helps with attentional processes, calculations and reading content such as instructions, and so we are in a proactive rather than reactive 'state', yet also, many other processes are still happening in the background that overlap neuroception, attachment and being safe in the worlds you are in, both corporeal and digital.

Therefore, we enter an academic difficulty when we try to impose, suggest or research our behaviour and activity within our multifaceted behaviours and underlying motives. *Our devices are both a tool and a medium,* and whilst we are looking into the screen, our messengers can become confused as they are not perceiving real-world visceral feedback in the way that we do when facing someone, something or some event in the real world. Looking and living through a screen can fool the brain, but can it fool the body?

I haven't included here the immersive technology of **virtual** and **augmented reality** and how this is likely the next level of changing and/or confusing landscape for our biology. That's the next project on my list of exploration and curiosity (although I have written about this already on blogs). Technology is increasing the way we can communicate and sabotaging how we communicate at the same time. Our biology is becoming confused, or is it? Do we even have the answers if we don't know the questions? And is virtual reality more similar in transactions and processes to the real world than staring 'into' or through a screen? Will our biology be more comfortable with one form of technology than another? And what happens when we begin to integrate technology into our biology such as systems being set up by Elon Musk or Openwater? Are technologies based on the TV series *Black Mirror* the next step?

To give you an example of what the preceding questions may look like when synthesised with theory and practice, imagine the following: Mum looks adoringly at baby and smiles.★ Baby receives this information through their eyes and is being held gently, 30 to 40 cm from Mum's face and close to her heartbeat. Baby feels safe★ (all pathways are operational, and the baby is in the green lane). The baby returns a smile to mum and coos★. Mum, also feeling safe★, then returns that coo, and the relationship between Mum and baby feels good for both★, and all is well in the internal subjective worlds of both Mum and baby. (★ Oxytocin secreted.)

Now imagine that the baby is being held slightly more upright, like a phone/smartphone, iPad, laptop or, well, you get the idea. We gaze into the screen at an image of our loved ones or friends (or kittens) or read a post on social media that is to our liking, and we feel like the baby in the last few sentences. We are perhaps gorging on finding oxytocin through the screen.

Now consider the older child on their way home from school. Not only is the device consuming the attentional processes of a human mind/brain and body whilst they are engaged in its contents; orienting responses, cognitive load and pattern recognition, attentional cues, reward circuitry and social circuitry (to name a few processes) are all also being pulled on simultaneously from within the device, and yet our biology will be trying to do the same with our environmental cues, which is perhaps why we can struggle to prioritise one domain over the other. We find ourselves checking in and out of our environment, and perhaps not giving it the due diligence, it deserves, or we omit to pay any attention to it whatsoever. They miss their bus stop or walk into a lamppost or off the kerb and so on. (This is a very important factor as to the issues of driving and texting/talking.)

Is your mind capable of fully attending to two worlds simultaneously? Where I often speak of online and offline being merged and having no separation nowadays, perhaps we are looking at the **neuroplastic** changes that mean we will evolve to manage two worlds simultaneously and perhaps not. Who knows, when it comes to the changes taking place in our world because those very changes are so rapid that we may not have time to research and fully understand before the next 'installation' and upgrade?

Brain waves and 'the program, the default and the sponge'

This section is a developing area of our knowledge, and so some of the research is still in its infancy stage, some is difficult to prove (as was attachment theory when it began) and some is conjecture yet still worthy of consideration. The actual science behind **brain waves**, measuring them and using them for recovery or performance changes is becoming a much better understood intervention and area of research, yet I would caution readers to hold some of this section lightly, remain open to possibilities and, of course, think critically about what I refer to. I am open to the prospect of being incorrect and being okay with this; however, if science begins to find that the following section is indeed supported, then we need, as a society, to really consider what our children are doing in and around technology, pronto.

A brain wave is an electromagnetic frequency that we can actively measure to show what is happening internally in the brain with the electrical circuitry (neurons in the brain communicate with electrochemical signals). In the laboratories, scientists often carry out experiments and measure the results using electroencephalogram (EEG) sensors. We can measure the brains responses to certain stimuli such as pain, heat, visual stimulation and so on. We will look briefly at the senses of sight and sound in relation to watching/using technology.

Our brain moves between these states depending on what we are engaged with at that time, and some scientists suggest this is also influenced by our age/stage of development, and children soak up information in certain brain wave states without critically questioning the validity or evaluation of the information. However, this is still considered contentious and requires a much deeper level of enquiry than I can actively cover here. Let's undertake that it is possible (yet needs deeper research). Verny and Kelly (1982), Dispenza (2010), Lipton (2015), Wolynn (2016) and many, many more suggest the environment has an impact on our biology from 3 generations back to today's world (**epigenetics**), and as a result, we have an unconscious 'program' that we then 'run' similar to an operating system (the computer metaphor here is helpful). In transactional analysis, we call this patterning a script, rather like the written script of a play. I am using brain–wave state and age examples here to give you a brief overview on this subject matter, although to date, I have no real, robust, long-term evidence of the claims. The jury is currently out on the age/stage conversation. Time will tell.

So what are brain wave states, and what does this mean?

Think of a ladder, with each rung representing a level of what we are doing with our brains at the time. During the day, we adults have 'states' of being, such as waking, sleeping, alertness, relaxed or deep concentration. So let's look at the rungs of the ladder as levels akin to a computer game. The ages/stages section may well be a red herring until we can find a way to robustly support and research this. I am sure technology will advance enough in the next 50 years to be able to do this "on the move", so to speak, rather than lying, standing or sitting in or with machines and wires.

An addendum to Table 5.1 is the state known as gamma: This state, whilst mapped out on paper, looks to be above high beta waves in terms of frequency does not map out in terms of behaviour. For example, if gamma is a higher state than high beta (anxiety), this must mean gamma is utter panic? However, research shows that this state is far from an anxiety-inducing experience. It is a state reported to be infrequently reached and is referred to as the bliss state, the feeling of unison with the world and can sometimes be called the 'aha' state when we suddenly gain insight into a puzzle. Unless we are well-practised and meditative monks or we spend time in the 'flow' or at peak performance, we may not recognise

Table 5.1 Brain wave states and childhood summarised

Brain Wave State	Characteristics	Hz (cycles per second)	Proposed Ages/Stages Important note: The author can find no evidential studies for the stages named in this column
Delta	This is when we are asleep and dreaming. This state is often present in children/adults with developmental trauma.	0–3	0–2
Theta	This is the deep, relaxed state we are in when we are meditating, daydreaming, almost asleep and alternative states of consciousness (hypnogogic trances). This state is where imaginary friends often appear (magical thinking).	4–7	2–5 years
Alpha	This is our relaxed semi-conscious/semi-awake state when we are listening to music, radio, watching TV and taking in information without judging it. It bypasses our critical thinking, i.e. our 'Oh really?' circuitry. This is also the state we can be in when we have watched a whole box set on Netflix without moving (and have numb limbs, e.g. lying awkwardly for an hour) and you can why perhaps young children become 'fixated' with TV/images on screen if this is what it feels like to be 'engrossed yet not aware of your surroundings'. Note: It can also be said, and this here is my opinion [The Author]; that there is enough visual stimuli to keep our brains entertained in terms of novelty and repetition with having to exert that cognitive load to process. This may only encompass a few genres of media, though action sports and music videos compared with media that involves concentration for the story line such as a crime thriller, and perhaps alpha brain waves vary in intensity also. The cusp of the next stage (beta) might be where our cognitive load is a little more focused on working out what happens next in the storyline rather than 'mind-numbing media.	8–11	6–10 years approx.

(Continued)

Table 5.1 (Continued)

Brain Wave State	Characteristics	Hz (cycles per second)	Proposed Ages/Stages *Important note: The author can find no evidential studies for the stages named in this column*
Beta (low to high)	Beta is our awake phase where we pay attention to the information and think about it. We are cognising our world and assessing the information for valence and value. We ignore what we are not really interested in. It is the critical analysis of incoming information, and we can be in this stage when we are reading, talking and debating. This is our *thinking clearly* state. **AND/OR** High-range beta waves tend to be associated with excessive analysis or over-attention on the information, and this ties into the fight/flight feelings we discussed earlier. This high range is the state often measured in neurofeedback of people with anxiety and excessive worry. Note: Considering the high-range beta stage does not necessarily mean high anxiety, it is perhaps a separation/overlap of the states through maturation that can be attributed to young people feeling anxious around these ages? Adolescence, around 12 years old, creates the ability to think critically as children move towards adulthood, and so this may be the age when separation and movement in and out of wave state 'levels' sits alongside the brain development of the emerging adult and why anxiety about life, friends and self is more apparent.	12–35 Approx. zones of beta: Low: 12–15 Mid: 15–18 High: 18–36	10+

Source: Fisher (2014)

this state in our daily life/practice as often. Richard Davidson spent many years researching this topic and has reported on his test subject Matthew Ricard (known as the happiest monk alive), who was observed in this state in the functional magnetic resonant imaging machine both very quickly and for an extended period. It is suggested that to become this masterful at moving into gamma and staying there takes approximately 40 years to perfect. Many of us humans may only experience this state for brief moments, and it can be the state we chase in relation to altered states of consciousness (Goleman & Davidson, 2017).

Brain wave states and devices

When we use our devices, we can be engaged in technical activities (beta) or we can be engaged in watching a low cognitive-load video on social media (alpha), mindlessly scrolling through our feeds (alpha), and only when we need to attend to an article, image, or text do we pay attention (beta). These activities may overlap, and we may find ourselves wandering off in thought as we face our device (theta). We may see something that captures or primes our attention, for example our name (the cocktail party effect). We may zero in on the post (convergent vision and fight/flight and higher levels of beta) and may be presented with negativity, shock or confusion, which now moves us higher in receptivity and focus (high beta). We may need to complete an action in this state to return to low beta or alpha, such as a tut, laugh, movement or, indeed what often happens in social media spaces, a comment, emoticon or valance(-like) reaction.

Through many years of speaking to my clients, they suggest that once you have been evoked, provoked or shocked by something you see on social media, without warning and, of course, something that you are scrolling past (mindlessly in alpha state), you may well be jarred from that post, video or image for some time after the fact by suddenly 'remembering' it. This is a simple description of my suggestion of what cybertrauma is.

As we currently do not have any robust (longitudinal) research showing robust brain-wave states of people interacting daily with their social media, apps or content, we are currently using our 'best guess' about what is happening with users of devices. Although underpinned by research around trauma, stress, social and cognitive psychologies, we are still somewhat in the dark. We are meandering through the land of correlation and attempting to attribute causation to many of these cumulative micro-moments of a person's activity with social media or devices. So, when you read about the causes of social media, gaming or devices and mental health issues, you can certainly take the current propositions with a pinch of salt.

What about the children?

This means that when we take a meta-look at this, for children younger than 12 using this brain wave state research, that they do not have the ability or capacity to filter out information in a mature, critical way, unless we as the adults are their regulators of this information, and this requires us to be the critical thinker in order to do so. We must be the expert of our own minds, self-aware of our own emotional temperature and can monitor, measure and future think about the content our children see, interact with and passively absorb. What I can say from many years of working with young children in therapy is that the stories they reveal in play are direct parallels to their corporeal lives and young children absorb almost every narrative presented to them by family and society without question. In transactional analysis, we call this the life script.

Children will 'take in the environment' through the experiences of observing, images, sounds, conversations and rules (explicit and implicit), and they 'become their environment' in terms of thinking, feeling and doing. This is the architecture of the developing human, and the blueprint is becoming increasingly complex as it spans corporeal, virtual and highly immersive areas together. Their brains operate on a permanent mode of taking it all in, sifting and discarding what does not serve you and using what allows you to survive in this family, village or world. What information are they taking in whole, what do they discard or not understand and what becomes their daily bread of what society looks like when informed by algorithms, information, **misinformation, disinformation** and non-critical thinking?

Moving to an established theory of online behaviour

If all the preceding, from attachment to motivation to brain wave states and child development stages are true, then a well-respected piece of research pertaining to online behaviours now explains a secondary aspect of human behaviour online and through technology rather than the primary focus.

Several years ago a researcher called John Suler (2004) proposed that the underlying reasons of our behaviour online are due *to the **online disinhibition effect*** (Suler, 2004). This is often taught to cyber-psychology students, therapists and people who work remotely (online) as to what they need to consider about a person's change of behaviour when using digital technology. The main proposition, according the author, is (paraphrased) as 'people vary in their disinhibition across a continuum from benign to toxic and many of the principles have their root in cognitive processes, alongside affective clusters' (the author is referring to emotions/feelings here). The author suggests that the six factors interact with each other and personality factors can influence this process.

It sounds complicated, doesn't it, because perhaps you have just read that there is a continuum and lots of other factors can impact this issue? To expand on the statement about personality factors, this is an area of vast discussion that further complicates this issue. For the sake of this reflection here, let's say that we take the most popular theory of research on personality factors known as the Big 5 or the Five Factor Model (Costa & McCrae, 1988). This relates to five further continuums of each factor creating a very large set of contiuums.

This, in short, means the online disinhibition effect is made up of one major continuum of benign to toxic, with six factors (each also a continuum) interplaying with five further continuums. That's a lot of possible outcomes or motivations of human behaviour. If this were mapped out in a diagram or graph for you, there would be many axes, and this would likely be very confusing for us all. However, simply put, that's a lot of possible reasons as to why a human might do what they are doing online. *This is an extremely important point to note.*

Suler's theory also suggests the polemic nature of both benign and toxic systems. For example some people will use the online space to explore parts of themselves perhaps to achieve what is called 'self-actualisation' in humanistic psychology (meaning to grow to be your best self). They may share parts of themselves and be kind to each other. This seems to suggest that people are using it for positive aspects, using it to explore and resolve internal processes and affect personal growth, yet the language infers negativity or a lack of active curiosity, motivation and energy. I wonder if the word conjures up for some readers a benign tumour image. It certainly did for me and a feeling of deficiency or absence of my humanness. Suler's theory could be read to suggest your YouTube, Netflix and social media habits here as potentially benign. Do you consider this about your behaviour to be true?

Traits that require much more self-awareness, self-development, compassion, focus and drive, in terms of investment in one's growth and prosperity, seem to have a flavour of positivity, and so the word *benign* doesn't sit with me comfortably in this sense. My clients in therapy invest heavily in themselves, whether that's confronting pain or having defences to keep themselves safe, so nothing about the process feels benign. As a side note, those who invest only in themselves perpetually (often called narcissists) may well be using the digital space to further this sense of self, whilst appearing at this end of the continuum? And so would we not need to know the need, the why and intent behind their motivation and subsequent behaviour before suggesting what they post, visit or observe online as a classification?

The toxic end of the continuum suggests that people are trying out behaviours that may be negative that they would not necessarily do or say in public or with other human beings present. Yet some of this behaviour may well be an attempt at reclaiming power, agency and autonomy from a child or adult who has previously been powerless or may be an attempt to explore risk-taking as an adolescent, you know the 'trying it on' phase that we often see in young children too? Yes, recipients of this behaviour can say it is toxic, but can we really say this about the earlier example?

As you have been reading thus far, bodily perceptions, called neuroception drive much of our behaviour around others in social situations. You may well have noticed that I am suggesting through the previous chapters that biological processes drive some of the disconnection that occurs with device use and enhances that false safety, which is where I'm suggesting this is the underlying foundation of why we have the disinhibition effect. The body comes before affect and cognition, and therefore, the online disinhibition effect is secondary to the biological processes of neuroception, false safety and information processing (brain waves) in and around device use.

References

Costa, P., & McCrae, R. (1988). From catalog to classification: Murray's needs and five factor model. *Journal of Personality and Social Psychology, 55*, 258–265. https://doi.org/10.1037/0022-3514.55.2.258

Dispenza, J. (2010). *Evolve your brain: The science of changing your mind.* Health Communications Inc.

Fisher, S. (2014). *Neurofeedback in the treatment of developmental trauma: Calming the fear-driven brain.* WW Norton & Co.

Goleman, D., & Davidson, R. (2017). *Altered traits: Science reveals how meditation changes your mind, brain, and body.* Avery Publishing.

Lipton, B. (2015). *The biology of belief. Tenth anniversary edition. Unleashing the power of consciousness, matter and miracles.* Hay House.

Suler, J. (2004). The online disinhibition effect. *Cyberpsychology and Behaviour, 7*(3), 321–326. https://doi.org/10.1089/1094931041291295

Verny, T., & Kelly, J. (1982). *The secret life of the unborn child.* Sphere.

Wolynn, M. (2016). *It didn't start with you: How inherited family trauma shapes who we are and how to end the cycle.* Penguin Life.

6 Addiction, attachment or something else? What is the problem?

Introduction
Are we addicted to technology, smartphones, gaming, social media or the internet?

Why it 'looks' like technology/social media or **gaming addiction** on the surface, but rarely is a pathological addiction diagnosis. Reading, watching or interacting with a line of text, an image or a video is not the same as a line of cocaine, bottle of wine or sexual gratification. Quite the question, hey? Have you noticed that we use this terminology in everyday life to cover many things that we like? In therapy, my clients often tell me how addicted they are to: shoe shopping (after payday), TV shows which have predicted endings, make-up/beauty products which have 'cured' their blemishes and more. Of course, none of them are 'pathologically' addicted to these products or things (as you'll see later), but it is common to use the word in a way that denotes you really, really, really like something, which is not addiction in line with Psychiatric diagnoses. Often, this happens with the word *depressed* too when people talk about not being able to buy the shoes, watch the TV program or find their blemishes have returned. Yet they often mean saddened, frustrated, annoyed and fed up and not Clinical Depression. Language matters, and therefore, this is so important here.

I think it would be helpful for you to understand the difference between these everyday versus pathological meanings. I'm going to provide an example taken from a blog, citing a research journal article and a mainstream media article in which the contributors have addiction or gambling clinics. I highlight some of my thinking around the terms and then move to a more compassionate definition of addiction and discuss behaviours of addiction afterwards. A point of note is the differences of substance, gambling, sex and addiction to the internet/gaming and social media typologies, and I intend to pick these apart for you.

DOI: 10.4324/9781003169390-7

A blog written in 2016 begins with an explanation as to what digital devices enable users to do; the author describes the internet as a place of communication and the sharing of information (Wright, 2016). I am hoping that you have asked the question, What about the benign disinhibition effects of watching videos, reading or accessing programs to help you carry out your work? Digital addiction to both the internet and texting is then discussed with the characteristics laid out as a list with no explanation of whether all or some of them need to be present at the same time. I will name these in a moment as areas to consider separately with a discussion surrounding each one. The blog names some academic research pointing towards adolescents' use of the internet as an addiction by Durkee et al. (2012), so again this cannot be generically applied outside of this context. And a further mainstream article is discussed within the blog (Swanson, 2014), which, upon reading, begins with a paragraph about texting and driving, a proposition to discuss texting addiction and internet disorders as encompassing all online behaviours. The contributor is the founder of a centre for internet addiction, and so I wondered how they will treat a person with this named disorder if it covers *all* online behaviour. To highlight the critiques of these approaches I need to challenge each of these characteristics.

Compulsive use of the device

I wonder how this is measured in terms of, say, a child needing to do their homework using a computer/tablet and how compulsively driven they would be to actually use that device if schoolteachers have directed them to do so? (or has happened in lockdown 2020). Or a businessperson also needing it to do their work outside the office and having a deadline to meet? I wonder if the authors of the research were considering compulsive use of entertainment based processes such as games or social media platforms via the internet rather than the device itself? In this case, the definition here could do with specifying what kind of behaviour this related to, and of course what the compulsiveness measurements/scales would be if one were to diagnose this.

A preoccupation with being online

I wonder if this term is old hat now as the smartphone and internet are always on and we are always connected. How would a young person define online? Anecdotal evidence and conversations on my podcast suggest they do not see smartphone use as online. How would the researchers define the young people talking 'online' to their friends, leaving a group chat for example to go and eat their meal and now they are thinking about the next time they can use their device to rejoin the conversation? Are they preoccupied in an addiction sense or group cohesion and belonging? Have you ever spent the day preoccupied with whether you should phone someone; maybe a partner or a friend, or make a business call? Do you have telephone addiction?

You see when a human becomes preoccupied with something, it can also look like a passion, a remembering or perhaps a desire to complete something like a task on a list. The description of preoccupation that overwhelms or takes the place of all other thoughts, sounds more like a pathological issue, such as a rumination or obsessive and intrusive thinking. Realistically, who are we to say that how much someone thinks about something is excessive, and in comparison, to what? What would happen if, for one of my clients who was the carer of his terminally ill father, the only time he could 'switch off' from thinking about the impending death was to be socialising with his friends? Does he have an addictive, morbid preoccupation with death during the day? Most likely, he is preoccupied as he looked at his father each time he entered the room and saw his skeletal body, frail posture and ever-increasing inability to hold a cup, chew his food or speak. He has no choice other than to be preoccupied with health and death right now.

His way to forget this is to become occupied or distracted with something else, like being online with his friends and, in his words, 'being a normal kid'. It is important to note here that being occupied or distracted are techniques we employ as human beings to face away from something horrible, and these are often known as defences in the psychological literature, and why wouldn't you want to defend from horrible feelings?

In this case, it is likely my client would have received a pathological diagnosis, not for his avoidance of persistent thoughts about his father dying but the preoccupation of when he could next 'go on Minecraft'; this obsession or compulsion (pathology-based words) or desire and need (humanistic and compassionate words) to be online is what he talked about at school, whereupon the teachers referred him to me for this 'incessant conversation above all else'. Yes, my client would often talk in lessons about Minecraft rather than doing his maths, and you know what, I feel I would too! His pain was so deep that he was trying his best to cope. I saw him as a superhero who had found a way to beat his kryptonite. He needed tenderness and compassion and not a diagnosis or label.

Would we say thinking about something a lot was a healthy preoccupation, distraction, distress-tolerance technique and when would we not? Sometimes, for some people, the preoccupation is a soothing technique to their distress, and it's about trying to feel safe and get back in the green lane.

Lying or hiding the extent or nature of the internet use

I question how the researchers know the respondents are telling the truth about lying (even when self-reporting) or when their partners or parents indeed report the other person as lying? This approach has been taken from the substance misuse literature and interventions in which you can evidentially 'see' if someone has drunk a bottle of alcohol and denies this or is high on substances and again denies this as being true. And so, if for example a child was to use their device at night, post an image on social media, or you could monitor the use of devices in real time (which you can), you would have concrete 'evidence' that they were on their device if they were to then tell you that they were not. However, if you suspected use of a device and there was no trace of activity, would we then be in a situation in which there is no 'proof' of use, and this could result in a battle of 'truth telling', and this can even present itself in my therapy room as events that are even 'phantom', whereby partners and parents tell me of device/social use that they suspect is occurring and yet isn't always the case. Lying is a complicated phenomenon, and we cannot prove it robustly, yes even with the polygraph (lie detector).

Use, the nature of use and the extent of use we have covered already in the explanation about the motivation, intent and needs a person has in their why, and of course, I can see that a user (over 18) of adult sites may well be embarrassed for someone to see their internet history and know they have visited these sites; however, can we classify a small number of visits and hiding this as addiction versus the person who visits many times and does not care who knows? Secrecy and therefore, at times, the covering up of the truth are about staying away from shame, and more often than not, when we find the 'evidence' of someone lying, we use it punitively in a psychological game of 'Now I've got you son of a bitch' (known as NIGYSOB) (Stewart & Joines, 1987). It's no wonder people try to hide what they consider shameful experiences from others.

Craving to spend more time online

I think this one speaks for itself in terms of cravings for feelings of desire, longing and wanting. We crave relational connections in many ways. We can crave something we don't have, would like, are allergic to or have a deficiency in, such as the cravings pregnant women get. As many of us can attest, cravings can also subside and are not necessarily the same as an intrusive persistent thought; they are fleeting feelings about wants and needs. Cravings are difficult to separate from a genuine/authentic need versus a liking of something and require a conversation to elicit much more information about this act.

Secretive behaviour (regarding online use)

As mentioned secretive behaviour is always linked to shame. Perhaps a young person is curious about a topic or something that they don't know, and this may result in secretive behaviour. For example, you can ask (Google) something, and it can give you an answer without humiliation. Furthermore, secrecy and privacy are normal parts of relational behaviour. We keep things private from our loved ones, such as thoughts, urges, desires, fantasies, present buying and, again, not wanting to look stupid. This is a shame/rejection and humiliation prevention technique. For example, a young person may want to know what a word means that heard their peers use, for example *snogging* (meaning kissing). Before googling it, the young person would likely say that they understood a word to prevent humiliation. Now they can find out without fear of retribution, ridicule or feeling stupid in front of others – and 'secretly' whilst with them if they are using a smartphone.

Keeping your use and what you 'do' online secret from friends and family may well be directly linked to identity formation, sexuality, exploration and curiosity and, of course, having interests and hobbies you don't want others to know about. The secrecy is an avoidance of shame. If the person trusted those around them not to do this, would they need to keep it secret? If you're in the blue or red lanes, this is going to be very difficult to regulate, and so secrecy is a sign of relational mistrust. Wouldn't we do well to ask questions and find out the motivations for a particular behaviour and respectively look to the context?

Could this be why internet browsing companies initiated incognito modes some time ago? And why didn't they call it secret mode? As I teach the children, I see through therapy that there are secrets that harm and secrets that create surprise and warm feelings of joy. We just have to look at the modus operandi to see what's behind the behaviour and the intended outcome of that behaviour. Secrecy is not always a 'bad' thing.

Mood swings

I think I can be brief here to say that mood swings reflect the mood we are in. Moods are very simply put a time of feeling a particular way.

States and traits are also time-based spaces, and we know that a mood can be short-lived but is not a trait such as depression. Food, temperature, substances, health and wellness can all affect mood as can the weather or what you spend your time thinking about or what has happened to you. Mood swings are likely for all of us and if you are being bullied online then you will meet some of the criteria in this article to potentially warrant a diagnosis of digital addiction. Which doesn't seem quite right for a pathological label?

So is it really addiction or not? Compassion, reflection and a humanistic approach

Now I am not saying that people cannot be and are not pathologically addicted to certain things; however, I argue about the why, how, when and function of these behaviours and, of course, whether digital, social media, gaming or Facebook addiction is the same as substance addiction.

In terms of definitions in and around the literature; I like, but don't fully agree with the one given by Gabor Mate, which, in short, says that addiction is a behaviour through which a person tries to allay, reduce or mitigate against painful feelings, and the person cannot stop or give up this behaviour even when there are negative consequences to that behaviour (Mate, 2009). I have reservations and queries about the negative consequences of the definition because is this the only time we call it an addiction? For example, if I am going to the gym to reduce my stress and I begin to get a defined physique, this would surely count as positive and healthy behaviour if I were slightly overweight to begin with. If I took time out of work to do this and then worked later in the day, would this be classed as flexible working hours or classified as a workaholic or gym addict? And, professionally, the digital behaviours I see have some, but not all, this negative behaviour. It's often a relational–emotional–regulation–seeking pattern, which we covered earlier in attachment behaviours.

In this respect, I ask, what are those consequences? Has anyone asked why the person engages in the behaviour in the first instance? What function does the behaviour serve? This is often the tell-tale motivator, and to be frank, I have often been informed by young people both in and out of therapy; the internet is a place to 'be' or hang out with their friends. Some have said that they are in a household in which they are bored or don't communicate with parents/siblings, and so they hang out with their friends online who may be geographically farther away than is possible to go outside and play with. We are back to attachment, peer relationships and belonging and, of course, needing seeking behaviours.

How difficult it must be to live in a family in which people don't or can't communicate with each other. This must feel very isolating, lonely and or neglectful. This must be very difficult for a child to manage, and perhaps, they will feel that they have 'done something wrong' or 'are bad or have a deficit in some way'. Given this line of thinking, wouldn't you want to hang out with other people? Wouldn't you be looking to find others who accept you and want to speak with you? And if you couldn't leave the house, online would be the way to go, no?

There is a (media-driven) piece of research that makes (quite grand) suggestions that the invention of the iPhone is to 'blame' for many of the ills and addictions our children face* (Twenge, 2017). There are books that suggest the internet has made us less able to operate in terms of memory and day-to-day functioning (Carr, 2011; Gazzaley & Rosen, 2016) and books that suggest we have outsourced our mental capacities so much that we suffer with digital dementia (Weiss, 2012), and of course, the debate about screen time is mixed in here too. It is also now in print to the new pathology of gaming disorder in the International Classification of Disorders volume 11 (WHO, 2019). For now, you can guarantee that you will see the word *addiction* used with and around devices, gaming and the internet, mostly by the mainstream media and in generic conversations from parents, professionals and non-academics who do not study or work with these issues. There are studies and some desktop research ideas emerging that show one neurotransmitter, one study, one area of the brain or one example and case study (usually a personal reflection) as the science, neurobiology and evidence of this issue and this is often the driving force to 'prove' addiction exists.

I would like to step in here as the writer and suggest that we need to look at all the evidence to weigh in on this debate, for which I am not entirely convinced that one or a few neurotransmitters, one study, one personal reflection or one/few areas of the brain's functions are entirely responsible for all (or some) of our behaviours. I find this reductionistic; it leans away from what it is to be human and dismisses the interplay of family, sociological factors, history, and psychology of the individuals and of course the motivations of the human desire to connect. In my practice, I acknowledge and revere neuroscience as a discipline and use these explanations to help clients understand themselves and create change, yet this is not the panacea of 'the why'.

Neuroscience 101 – it's much more complicated

When we look at brain scans of people with addictions, we see the areas such as the nucleus accumbens light up in the anterior (front) part of the brain. Neuroscientists will tell you this is about the neurochemical dopamine and the reward pathways here (Kandel et al., 2013). However, if we look at the regions in the brain that involve attachment seeking behaviour which also involves reward and motivational circuits, we can see similar physical areas in the brain being used, and of course, these overlap, so which is it: attachment, addiction, motivation or reward?

In short, the system for motivation and reward is also involved in connection and socialising. Now, in terms of how we interpret the data from brain scans, we can say that we know those areas are being 'used' at the time of scanning because they are either using oxygen or an injected dye, or we can see electrochemical signals between the areas. However, as much as I am a neuro-nerd and really do love this science, I am also sceptical for the following reasons:

> When I was sat typing this I wondered (as an engineer) if I could measure the electricity between the component parts in my computer and could I accurately predict what program the computer was running as I did so? (spoiler – the answer is no). However, if I went a little deeper and monitored the binary flow of information, could I 'decode' what was occurring within the computer? (This would more than likely be a large but doable task, and ironically, I would need a computer to help or translate this for me.)

Then I considered the issues of would I know WHY the program was being used, would I know who was using it or for what purpose? These answers are a definite 'nope' kind of moment, and here's the thing: our brains are much more complicated than any computer ever, in fact, probably more complicated than all the computers in existence, and here's the (*not-accurate) statistics: if we pretend for a moment that everyone has a computer, with current figures of the world population, we would be looking at almost 8 billion of them.

Now consider a baby's brain for a moment. There are estimated to be 100 billion neurons (estimated as we can't accurately measure these, and this figure is often thrown around at lectures and in literature). However, alongside every neuron are approximately 3 glial cells so that means 300 billion glial cells and 100 billion neurons each with a possible connection of *insert unknown calculation of numbers that seem impossible* = WOW!

Wow doesn't even cover it really, does it? So, as much as we can follow brain imaging techniques and accurately predict behaviours of humans in relation to specific locations and activity in the brain, we don't know very much. It's a little like predicting the weather; we know enough about the patterns to make predictions, but I've yet to see a 100% accurate forecast based on these systems. We humans are more complicated than these dopamine hits, reward and motivation circuits and behaviours that may seem to be based in the addiction narrative. When we look closer and talk with the gamer, there's a multifactorial, layered explanation.

I agree that we can be drawn towards behaviours through our habitual responses or reactions. This can create longing and desire, which can result in a feeling of a 'need' rather than genuine, authentic needs (this confusion is often what I help clients untangle in therapy). We are very complex beings, and I personally feel that we are much more than neurobiology, more than observable and statistical behaviours, and there needs to be much more phenomenological (a person's view of their experience) and subjective explorations into the fields of internet-, gaming-, pornography use-, shopping- and gambling-based research. Context, culture, family, time, history and individual perspectives need to be accounted for whilst also understanding that even this approach will omit important aspects of our behaviour. Multidisciplinary research and analyses are needed to understand complex human behaviours.

The issue with these media-driven articles is the way in which they are reported. They often drive a very scary doom-based massage so you will read their article. Hint: the evidence just isn't there yet, as we haven't had the internet long enough to make some of these claims; furthermore, as it changes so rapidly, research carried out in 1998 versus 2007 versus 2019 is all going to look very different as the technology was different, but negative stories sell right?

Why it looks like addiction and 'abnormal behaviour' in relation to gaming

In terms of the word addiction to devices, games, social media and its place in history, I hear this phrase used by parents, teachers or professionals from around 2015, when they want a child to engage in a particular behaviour and it is denied or ignored or when there is conflict. For example, a parent in the 1980s wants a child to put down the comic and put their shoes on for school. The child continues to walk across the room with the comic and the parent snatches it out of the child's hands, telling them they are obsessed with these darn silly things. A teen in the 1990s is using the house telephone, and after 30 minutes of talking, the parent wants to use the phone, telling the child, 'Get off the darn phone; you're glued to it!' or the child in the 2000s playing the Nintendo DS Nintendogs game and refusing to get ready for school or the parent saying to another in the yard, 'Couldn't get them away from the DS this morning; they're attached it!'

No hint of 'gaming/social media addiction' before this time, and it's not in common everyday language usage yet. I struggle to find articles in the media naming portable consoles as being addictive or associated with a disorder. I don't hear this phrase from parents or professionals in practice for a few years yet. I do however hear about the new fad in the playground causing tension such as Pokémon or Yu-Gi-Oh cards, Beyblades, flip phones, iPods, 'Super-Bluetooth' and 3G all being to become common issues.

As gaming consoles increase in prevalence, portability and popularity, devices become more affordable, the number of social media platforms increases, and smartphones are making an appearance. My therapy practice begins to become more focused on these conversations. I now hear parents using this *addicted* word. I hear children reporting that parents snatch the smartphones, consoles and devices away; cut plugs off or turn them off mid-game or -sentence; or hide them away for days and weeks as punishment and this results in the *behaviour that's often attributed to addiction.

This is where the everyday language has changed somewhat and now parents, teachers and professionals use the phrase addicted, rather than excited by or fanatical about. This, of course, seems to be associated with hobbies or sports only. We have created a system of blame and shame to appease adults who want their children, partners, friends, colleagues and others to conform and behave according to their wants and needs at the time of their demands. In non-violent communication (Rosenberg, 2001), demands and requests result in very different outcomes and interactions, and learning about this approach is more often than not the magic key for many of the parents I work with on this issue.

For now, however, have a quick think about when the word *addicted* gets used and if you could interchange it with something less pathological, shaming or insinuating a deficit or brokenness? Does this word appear when the person you are referring to isn't doing something you want right at that moment in time? Is this about them or us? This kind of reflection can be difficult for some of us.

References

Carr, N. (2011). *The shallows. What the internet is doing to our brains: How the internet is changing the way we think, read and remember.* WW Norton & Co.

Durkee, T., Kaess, M., Carli, V., Parzer, P., Wasserman, C., Floderus, B., . . . Wasserman, D. (2012). Pathological internet use among adolescents. *Addiction, 107*, 2210–2222. doi:10.1111/j.1360-0443.2012.03946.x

Gazzaley, A., & Rosen, L. (2016). *The distracted mind. Ancient brains in a high-tech world.* MIT Press.

Kandel, E., Scwartz, J., Jessel, T., Seigelbaum, S., & Hudspeth, A. (2013). *Principles of neuroscience* (5th ed.). McGraw Hill Medical.

Mate, G. (2009). *In the realm of hungry ghosts. Close encounters with addiction.* Vintage Canada.

Rosenberg, M. (2001). *Nonviolent communication: A language of life.* Puddledancer Press.

Stewart, I., & Joines, V. (1987). *TA today. A new introduction to transactional analysis.* Lifespace Publishing.

Swanson, J. (2014, June 10). The neurological basis for digital addiction. *The Fix* www.thefix.com/content/digital-addictions-are-real-addictions

Twenge, J. (2017). Have smartphones destroyed a generation? *The Atlantic.* www.theatlantic.com/magazine/archive/2017/09/has-the-smartphone-destroyed-a-generation/534198/

Weiss, M. (2012). *Digital dementia.* Self-Published fulfilled By Amazon.

World Health Organisation. (2019). *International classification of diseases for mortality and morbidity statistics. Eleventh revision.* https://icd.who.int/en/

Wright, C. (2016, April 22). Emails and the workplace. *Life Sciences.* http://scitech-connect.elsevier.com/email-and-the-workplace/

7 Parenting and professional understanding of children with, around and through technology

Introduction
Parenting before and after the appearance of technology, a skills-based reflection

A 3-year-old child is building a brick tower. Each time they get to the eighth brick, it topples. The child throws themselves on the floor and has a tantrum. Normal behaviour?

A 6-year-old is trying to pull out a stick from the game kerplunk, and each time they touch it and a ball falls, they pull the whole game to the floor, screaming that it's not fair and the game is stupid. Normal behaviour?

An 8-year-old child is playing on their computer and is involved in Pac-Man or Space Invaders requiring skills and expertise to advance to the next level. Just as the child is about to enter the final level and become champion, there is an electricity outage and the computer turns off. The child squeals in frustration, throws themselves on the bed and cries. Normal behaviour?

In all the preceding, I would say yes, this is what we call normal behaviour in terms of child development and emotional regulation skills. All the above are what we could expect from a child who is frustrated, angry and sad. Depending on their ability and capability to manage their feelings, we can expect that some of the reactions may be louder, longer and more distressed in some children than others, but we could say these would be normal reactions, all of which are certainly sounding like red lane behaviours!

So let's look quickly at what we (hopefully) do as parents or carers in this situation: the adult sits with the child and says, 'Hey, that's a terrible frustration, you must be so cross, and I understand how difficult, annoying, bothersome this is'. The adult really connects with the child and feels with them compassionately about all that effort and concentration

DOI: 10.4324/9781003169390-8

and knows this feeling. I'm sure you can rally a few examples up yourself about what this feels like. It's called frustration, having a hard time (a meltdown), and children are not very good at regulating their behaviour or emotions around this. We as adults help them learn to do this over time by connecting and regulating as described here. Children and perhaps some adults do not generally have the capabilities to be patient and internally regulated when feelings so big take hold of them. We have all been there, right?

A child with technology: now the child is 16. They are busy using their computer and have their headset on as they are playing a game with their friends online. This game is a **first-person shooter** (FPS) and requires the team to play a set of games and to win a flag. This means they must win consistently for several games (like sets in tennis). The 16-year-old is watching their **'head-up display'**, which contains lots of information to the game; they are talking to their teammates; they are following a constantly changing map; and they must change their weapons to defeat certain monsters or vehicles (requiring another screen momentarily). Mum has been shouting that dinner is ready for several minutes. The child has not heard this as they are 'in the zone or flow', wearing their headset and concentrating hard as this is the last game in the round. This is the round that could see them winning, gaining more points and respect from their online teammates. Mum is feeling frustrated about the dinner going cold. She walks into the child's room, announces loudly that dinner is ready and has been calling for 5 minutes and turns off the console. I'll leave you to consider what the response is from the 16-year-old! In terms of a response rated from calm to meltdown, I suspect you will have guessed at the latter end of this score, which begs me to ask why we inherently know this will be the response, yet the resounding issue brought to my therapy room is about the child or young person's reaction as being 'abnormal' and addicted to gaming? It seems rather unfair no.

The team player in the room and the team player online

After guessing the child would have likely displayed a meltdown response, here are a few possible reasons why that may have occurred in addition the sudden ending of the game. It's a little more complicated than frustration with not completing the game (like the brick tower example).

First, wearing a headset likely means the online players (both teams) will have been able to hear the shouting from Mum (unless the mic was off, although this is unlikely in a game of needed communication). The sudden disappearance of the player will have been noted by the online players. Although some players may be unknown, personally, it is likely that some of them are real-life friends or regular online teammates too, and of course, we have all had a situation in childhood like this being called in for tea in front of your mates.

Second, the young person's team were winning the match and close to the end of this game, and their departure may have cost their team the match. The player is left guessing if they are now responsible for their team's loss, only they were not the one who 'left' the gameplay through choice. They now spend the evening dreading going back online and, of course, facing some of their teammates at school the next day in case they are teased or bullied. What will they say? And will their teammates be forgiving? Should they take the day off school and feign illness? Cue an evening of worry, anxiety and anger towards the parent for not 'getting it' and shame when the parent tells them they are addicted, dismisses the importance of the game or calls it stupid.

This example is a scenario about a female client I saw in practice, not a male. I wonder if the image you had in your head as I told this story was of a male. I'm not going into stereotypes here; suffice to say that it is this kind of reporting that appears in the media, leading us to develop a belief about gaming addiction and who it mostly affects. These situations, highlighted in a news story without the full background, can look like a pathology if we don't consider the modus operandi, family dynamics, game of choice, impact on daily life and meaning-making behind the issue.

Why telephone addiction never existed, and why things are different now

An analysis of how it feels for a child or young person, as to why they find the sudden turning off the console, computer or game 'intervention' so distressful: This action carried out by the adult is having more of an impact compared to a 1990s' child using the phone for too long with their best friend. In this example, the parent might hang the phone up or pull the connector from the wall and the conversation would be halted between just two people – not two teams, a party or a stadium of players. The only person here to hear the background 'annoyance', and disconnection would be the friend on the phone. A very small audience and no sign of being told they have telephone addiction because they are talking to their friends using technology.

When a child has a headset on and switched on, the entire game can hear them as they communicate to their friends using technology. This may consist of a few or a few hundred other people. If the parent is speaking to or shouting at the child many players can also hear unless the child mutes the mic. This audience could consist of friends that may well tease, harass or bully the next time they play online together or at school or college the next time they meet. This is certainly the most reported issue young people discuss in my therapy room: how embarrassing, shaming or annoying this is to be teased the next time they play because their parent or carer was overheard, or the altercation was recorded and shared on other social media channels. This is one aspect of **cyberbullying**. And, of course, reactions to this at home may well underpin the diagnosis of gaming addiction or disorder.

An action like this, carried out in your house, may be akin to carrying this out in a public place, for example in front of the whole school or in the middle of a busy town? I wonder how many adults would feel comfortable with an audience like this. These games are often recorded by other team players, and I have seen bullying take this format when the videos are edited and the **gamertag** of the child can be identified, or parents call out to their children using first names because that's why we gave children names, right?

Parents are not deliberately intending to cause their child this level of distress. When I speak with them, they reflect a feeling of "I wish they'd listen to me and get off that game", and so they say this to the child, not knowing that the entire game may be listening. Because let's face it, you can't see the other players as you can on a football field or real-life activity. The child's reaction usually is "just a minute", and this is because they have a few things they now feel are imperative:

1   They need to save face and say goodbye to their friends in their own way/time.
2   They need to complete the level, play to ensure they or their team don't lose.
3   They need to ensure they keep their experience or gaming (XP) points, which often only get issued at the end of a game or at a save point.

To add further insult to injury, other gamers may tease the child and ask them to play hooky in the same way that a child is goaded into stay out late or stay off school, and this is a peer pressure that children have always encountered. However, I often find parents forget about this as they only see their child in their bedroom. It's almost like the 'others' do not exist and therefore are not held in the parent's mind when they ask their child to come off the device or game.

A reflection on our past: we as adults have our own childhood stories rooted in watching TV. While this was a passive activity, turning it off would not send out a notification to all our friends the instant it was turned off. This is not the case nowadays online when your online status suddenly disappears.

Why it can be a problematic issue and real case studies

Now if we look at a behaviour, that, in Japan since the early part of the 2000s, has been called **Hikikomori** (Teo & Gaw, 2017), these are (to date) males who haven't participated in society or shown a desire to do so for at least a year. This phenomenon is often attributed to gaming in the mainstream media, and we can see the narrative of young men staying in their rooms playing on their computers and 'holding the house hostage' in terms of not engaging with people, doing chores, cleaning themselves or going out to get a job. Would we say this was a gaming addiction or some other mental health issue? However, If I now switch to another angle, this looks like my client base who withdraw from face-to-face human connection which could be diagnosed as having autism spectrum disorder or depression in the Western world.

All the 'diagnoses' used earlier have the same 'symptoms' but a different precipitating factor, prognosis or treatment plan depending on the part of the world in which they are occurring or the culture in which they are found. However, if you take a closer look at Hikikomori, you can see that some of the young men spend their time reading, painting and generally avoiding contact with other people for many reasons. Some may be expressing behaviour that we as Westerners do not necessarily understand, yet we may well collate under the addictive diagnoses rather than social or cultural.

For example, in my practice, a young person who withdrew into their room to play games explained they were practising and building social skills without being in awkward public situations, just like a child would practise, rehearse or play football to improve their skills so when they play with their friends, they aren't the 'n00b' (a term used to mean useless beginner).

I have on occasion had to work with clients in therapy in which the gaming has indeed become a problem for that child within that family setting. This has taken on a case-by-case basis and approach as more often than I care to mention the gaming has become a way for that child to manage an aspect of their life, usually overlapping family, friends, school and an avoidance of something, and it is in this sense that I refer you back to the definition whereby the negative consequences can be seen here. The child I worked with did not shower, attend school or spend time with family members during their waking hours. After working with them for some time, it became apparent that they felt they were no good at anything in education, had low self-esteem and were showing signs of self-hatred and potentially an eating disorder developing as part of this issue. They were incredibly sad and felt alone. Gaming gave them a place to feel in company, albeit digital characters in this sense, and, of course, those they played the games with. There was little pressure to perform well in sports and pretend they were happy, and gaming allowed them to dissociate from the painful feelings.

Listening to my clients over the last decade, I have realised that this is a comprehensive explanation that uses many more cognitive processes than how we talk about addiction alone. It shows that they consider why they are doing what they are doing; it shows the potential to improve who they are, what they can do and where they want to be. Yes, a few of the children play games to be the next **YouTuber/E-sports** winner (see the gaming section in the book; Section II), and the only way to do this is to practice and rehearse, a lot. If we looked at football practice, we might say is about commitment rather than addiction, especially if your child is picked to attend a training school. One child explained that they were rubbish at maths/English and other subjects in school and that gaming was the only thing they excelled at, after some months of committed practice (which will nowadays likely meet the criteria for a gaming disorder); this allowed them to play and socialise with the other children who, in turn, then lessened their teasing. They felt like they belonged and could hold their own in the group.

Social psychology looks at 'in-group' dynamics and how we feel part of a tribe, collective or cohesive crowd and often concludes that it is how we see ourselves as part of that group. As children mature, their social identity and belonging become the focus and drive. This is considered a normative part of social, cognitive and psychological development. So why wouldn't they choose a group or space that was where their friends are?

So if we are not addicted what's the problem?

In terms of 'use', we don't have any clear guidelines about anything that exists to be honest, such as telephones, kettles or cars. We tend to rely on research, and when that fails to be communicated or understood, we are left with media reports and old wives' tales. Even when we have the research, it generally only gives us a snapshot for a certain cohort of people at a certain time, in a certain location in space and time.

To give an example and elaborate on this, take the guidelines we have about food. How often have you seen the same food group, for example coffee or tomatoes, being labelled as bad, good or cancer-causing? Where do you go to get good advice and guidelines? Well, 30 years ago, you went to the library and read about 'stuff', or you were told about it through the TV or friends (who get their knowledge from similar sources). In 2020, you probably googled it, saw it on the news or social media.

Either way, you are informed by another human being or machine learning algorithm with flaws and biases. Much like you are reading now, I am presenting some facts to you based on my previous learnings from research journals, books and life experiences (this includes other humans and a little bit of search engine findings). And here's where it gets 'human'; I can present you with ideas that you will either agree with or disagree with. I have no idea which choice you will make.

Screen time: the dreaded hypothetical construct with no validity

First, I need to introduce you to the idea or phenomenon of 'screen time' which is often quoted in the research and media in how we discuss children 'overuse' of devices or gaming. Let's call this the variable that we are going to research. In terms of keeping this book simple, I will remove my academic hat and say that this variable cannot be measured.

Think for a moment about what this means, a screen and the time spent at or looking at one. What does a screen constitute? A TV, computer monitor, smartphone, digital watch or ATM? A departures board at an airport, a cinema screen or a lecture whiteboard? Does it need to be colour, black-and-white, pixelated, inverted or a result of an image passed through tubes such as night-vision goggles or binoculars? (These both contain graticules, an optic scope which could be a screen within an item and one not considered till now).

How do we define the use of such screens? Is it glancing at, focusing on, staring at or towards it; passive or active engagement? How do we measure this time; do we ask a person who may not know or cannot say because they don't count (e.g. how many times we blink or sigh)? Do we install a monitoring device in their eyes so we can track this or follow a person around 24 hours a day taking notes about their eyes' activity? And, of course, when someone is watching something on TV for example are they using the screen for in their own thoughts and memories and their face just happens to be pointed at a screen? Sounds a bit ludicrous, doesn't it?

Ironically when neuroscientists are measuring what's happening in a person's brain through a functional magnetic resonance imaging machine, the participant is often looking at a screen whilst the tests are being administered. Do we count this as enforced screen time, and does this mean neuroscientists are abusing their participants? (This is a joke by the way, and the answer is no, but one to consider hey?) We could go on with silly examples, but I am sure you get my drift.

What about the apps or research in this area?

There are apps that can monitor when you activate, turn on or open your device (if it is locked) and which apps you use for how long; however, I noticed an issue with this personally when the app measured my podcast and listening time and counted this as screen time. I was certainly not looking at the screen whilst the podcast, audiobook or music played as it was in my pocket whilst I was out exercising. Accuracy matters when we try to measure things, and my screen time here was not a true reflection of my time using my device, and I had to do the maths, although it is rumoured that placing this app on a device may well be the get-out clause of someone 'suing' a device manufacturer. We very much, unfortunately, live in a litigious society.

Here's what research (currently) does, it asks people to report back on their technology use or the use of others such as their children. Now in terms of what we humans like to do when being asked about our (and our family) behaviours, we like to give 'socially desirable answers'. That is, we like to 'look good for the researcher'. So we skew our answers (a) so we feel better or worse about ourselves and (b) because we don't monitor our own behaviour that closely and make lots of errors in our responses. (So we give our best guess about what we think the researcher wants to hear.) We also do this at the doctors when they ask about a behaviour such as smoking, drinking, sleeping or peeing.

So here we have several issues on what screen time constitutes, what and how it is measured, and last, in 2020 how does this compare to, let's say, 2015 or 2010? When we see stories or courses that claim to reduce or improve screen time or end the parenting battles around them, we can perhaps now take a moment to think. What does this mean for me and others?

How can we make recommendations about screen time when we cannot define and measure it? How can we diagnose this as a disorder or suggest that excessive screen time (compared to what?) is the same or different to addiction? How do we measure apples against oranges? Also, it has taken me a long time to write this book, and I did so on a computer for which I stared at the screen for long periods – like really long periods – and for longer than a year. I am wondering if I need to seriously think about finding a detox clinic for my screen-based 'disorder'.

When is screen-based technology use a problem or disorder?

The word *disorder* has a negative connotation for most people as it denotes that someone is 'not normal' and dis-ordered. However, if we look at the word by moving our frame of reference to comedy for a moment, we can see that it means un-ordered, as in perhaps the famous quote by Eric Morecombe when playing the piano, and he suggests that he has all the correct notes but that they may not be in a correct sequence.

Each person is unique as is their family and friends, school, university and workplace. What might be an issue for one might not be for another. Perhaps when we look at the use of screens, devices, consoles or any other medium currently in use and on its way, we need to perhaps be more open to what this can, could and does mean for each family. When and how are what matter rather than what.

For example, I wrote in my first guidebook about a child I worked with who was so desperate to complete his online game campaign that he would often limit his drinking so he limited his urinating. He would hold his urine in for excessive times and would 'force' his urine out in a rush. Both issues are unhealthy in terms of how the body is designed to work. The impact of holding in your urine for a long time can result in muscles or kidneys not working as they should. This can be a temporary issue or result in permanent damage, both of which depend on a person's body which is unique. For this child, some succinct education about how his body worked provided him with a choice, with which he decided to support his kidneys and bladder muscles. He didn't want to take a chance on permanent damage. Other 'problems' may also be temporally transient (certain ages and time spans); for example the Hikikomori male is not listed as a 98-year-old man or a child younger than 12.

This suggests that perhaps, much like sports at school, certain screen-based technology apps and platform use may well be transient. We also know screen-based technology is here to stay, so we need to look at the content, context and modus operandi behind the use. We can see from stats released by internet social media companies that young people phase out of certain apps; for example Facebook is used less by young people, and Snapchat and TikTok are more popular. I believe that for many of us, we hit a saturation point with much of this technology, and when that occurs, we retract, reassess and consider our use of all forms of technology. We are, after all, drawn to the new and novel, and when this begins to wear off and become boring, we tend to leave it alone. It's why technology companies must consistently increase the way in which we interact to keep us interested.

We will always socialize, so the two issues will go hand in hand for some time yet. If we can work out our part in the process and consider if we are happy with our involvement, then perhaps this is a better way to look at our behaviour. For each person and their family, there may be an element of dis-order or negative consequences in and around this tech, so case by case, you decide if it's a problem for you or your family. And find a therapist who understands all sides of the debate and does not offer a magic bullet for a complex issue.

I don't deny the psychological tricks used by these companies to tap into our psychological insecurities to create more involvement with an app or platform, and I don't see this as addiction or a disorder. I see it as a manipulation of the human psyche for financial gains, and this looks more like a coercive and abusive relationship in which tech companies are the abusers. Is this a strong statement? Yes! And it comes from a background of sitting with people who are in these kinds of relationships, unaware of their slow drip, drip, drip change into the abused. And, of course, the abuser will deny that they are doing this, or they will feign any knowledge of this happening.

Can tech companies do better than tap into the humanness of humans and manipulate the essence of connection and belonging? Yes, they can. Will they? Perhaps. One of the approaches I see evolving is the ethical nature of challenging tech companies and looking at what we do with our time online, such as the organisation that Tristan Harris has created: X. The formulae for this require compassion, empathy, true connection, kindness, tolerance and transcendence above our differences, using an underpinning of humanistic psychology X rather than using technology alone to fix issues that people created with and through technology.

It's a tool and a medium

In summary, I think, feel and have noticed through many years of watching as a parent, clinician and researcher that the most reported motivating factor of screen-based technology use is to connect with other people. For example, gamers want to game with their friends. Social media platforms provide a way for us to connect with friends, families and colleagues or potential connections (e.g. jobs, business deals or dating). This is the main, but not elite, reason for using this technology, just as is using the telephone for calling someone. The other motivating factors are from wanting to carry out a behaviour, that is to do something 'there' (in digital or cyberspace).

Our technological devices are both a medium and a tool. They are the spaces we use for connecting to others and the *things* we carry out behaviours *on, through or with*. These devices facilitate two overlapping processes of being human interfaced with a screen to be in the digital space which you do not have in corporeal transactions as the other person is right there in front of you. (Virtual reality may change some aspect of this process in due course.)

So how do you parent when you and your children are operating in two worlds and within two processes simultaneously? How do you meet them where they are? These are questions to be answered throughout the rest of the book!

Reference

Teo, R., & Gaw, A. (2017). Hikikomori, a Japanese culture-bound syndrome of social withdrawal? A proposal for DSM-V. *Journal of Nervous and Mental Disease, 198*(6), 444–449. doi:10.1097/NMD.0b013e3181e086b1

Section II

Gaming: pitfalls, positives and processes

How to help

8 Gaming: good, bad or the problem? From play to time limitations

Introduction
So what about the issues that arise in or with gaming?

What about the positives? Why do children (or adults) game? Play. There I said it. A one-word child reply to the biggest question for this section. It is far more complex than this, as I have alluded to in the previous section, and of course, you would need to ask a child about their reasons, for which they cannot explain all of them in our language and so often say, 'To play'. Very simply, I will explain that play is an extension of learning, a space to explore, imagine and be creative, a brain architecture scaffold, a social, emotional and sometimes physical playground, a non-sensical purposeless process, a specific outcome or goal-orientated process, infinite and finite, a flow-based space, temporal vacation, self-discovery and mastery and, most important, a fun activity. A very good book on this subject matter explains play in detail (Brown & Vaughn, 2009) and far too many other authors to name here on the topic of play.

Here is a list of some of the things I find with my clients in therapy when using computer gaming: skills in areas such as sharing, motor control, reflexes, pain management, mindfulness, breathing techniques, anxiety and fear management, planning, reasoning and critical thinking, diagnostics, human behaviour, communication, peripheral vision, acuity, balance, dancing, musical appreciation, rotational imagery, judgements, memory, embodiment, groupthink, learning (all forms including reading, spelling, arithmetic, etc.), teamwork, connection, social skills, emotional support, identity formation, appreciation of art, programming skills, time management, noble defeat and how to play and have fun.

Pretty cool, huh? There are lots more than I have listed here with in-depth explanations, so please see the books listed for further reading. There is a lot to be said about games, their outcomes and how they

DOI: 10.4324/9781003169390-10

are another format of play which is the fastest way for a child to learn through trial and error. It's the quickest way for most of us to learn anything, hence the idea behind 'gamification' of almost all our life goals. If you don't know what I mean, have a quick think about how you compete with your friends to have the best car, house or gadgets? How you might enjoy the satisfaction of finding a free car parking space or getting into one just before that other person does? It can be something we don't even know we are doing and is often a feeling of competitiveness or of doing better next time. For example, the game that many people play with their satnav, the 'Can I beat the eta?'

So the same goes for children and young people who are playing games to better their skills. Games are interactive and immersive and have factual and fantasy elements; they bring about a narrative in story form, which means that we are captured by their essence as a 'bookworm is to the word'. Games can provide more than a book in terms of a child's success in the world. They observe the hero in a book and, in gaming, can be the hero or play a part in their success and victory.

As a therapist who works with and observes children suffering adversity, difficulties and struggles, it is a privilege and amazing moment to see them succeed at a game, puzzle or level within a game and for us to celebrate this. Sometimes celebrating it looks like they have won the Olympics because this is how 'big' it can feel to the child.

Children who are often stuck in low socio-economic-status lifestyles, care systems and a world in which there is so much pain for them often need a refuge that can be provided for and by a computer game. Lego Star Wars can be as satisfying, redeeming and helpful for a child as Fortnite is for another. It's all about the child's perception of the game they play, why and with whom they play and what they can achieve within or from it.

Some of the children I work with play games for an entirely different reason, this being experimentation without shame. They can fantasise and/or become the figure in the game, and they can experiment with who they are. Fantasy is about imagination and interaction with things that do not exist such as dragons, elves and witches (although I'm sure I know a few). Games allow for fantasies to emerge safely and within the control of the child, such as fighting an opponent to the death. For example, I loved playing Tekken for this reason; it meant I could play-fight and turn my ninja skills (which I don't possess) into a full-on rage at an imaginary figure. Through a process of catharsis, humour and button-tapping frenzies, I can rid myself of my frustrations of the day.

All humans have these thoughts and desires and whilst many of us adults can rid ourselves of them as quickly as they arrive (because you know punching your boss doesn't usually end up in high score points). It is through moral development and emotional regulation that a child learns. This occurs within play and acting out and is best supported by an adult who explains why it's not helpful to hit, bite or kick other children.

Empathy and compassion

Have you ever thought about games and how they can help a child learn about morals, values, fairness and compassion? You are likely to consider here that games have been described by many parents as causing less compassion and 'more anger outbursts'. Children (and adults) seem to love cartoons. There is something charming, immersive and delightful about them. This is likely due to the configuration of eye size and features of the characters that resemble babies, as we are naturally drawn to look after these 'tiny people'.

As we watch a cartoon, we begin to project onto, personify or anthropomorphise the figures we are watching, feeling their sorrows and pain when tragedy, rejection or pain inflicted on them. This is due to us having mirror neurons, and it means that we identify with that figure in the same way as another human. (Cozolino, 2006) In my practice, when I talk with the children about their game use, the following statements have been used to highlight how it is when considering compassion and empathy:

> Well, I wouldn't do that to my real friend as it's not fair and they wouldn't be my friend anymore.
>
> It's against the law, so like I know I can do it in the game because it's not real. It's not like people get hurt in GTA [Grand Theft Auto] but I know they would if it was like my dad's car or somat.
>
> You can get headshots and throw knives, but I would never do that, even in the real army (*meaning The Cadets) cos it's awful.
>
> Omg I would just die if someone did that to me or my mates and I'd want proper revenge for it like cos it's like against what's normal? Don't you think?

All these statements were from children younger than 12. As I asked the children what it would be like if this was real life, these were the follow-on comments:

> I just wouldn't, I bet it would make them cry so I wouldn't.
>
> Not a chance, my mum would kill me and anyway I could kill someone cos I don't know how to drive and that would be dangerous.

I wouldn't want to really shoot someone because there would be blood and I'd be sick and then I'd feel awful for killing them and my mum would have to wash my clothes from the sick and she would be mad at me and I don't like upsetting her, she is really sad cos of dad so I wouldn't make her more sad.

That'd be like trashing their house and can you think what that'd be like, I bet it would be like those trucks in France who drive over the tents of them people and just leave them with no home . . . urgh . . . awful.

Now I could safely put my money on these being the children's reflections of empathy, compassion, care, morals, values and fairness and distinguishing between play and reality. You see 'play' is a way to play with and around known and unknowns, which may sound like I have just written a riddle; however, this simply means, it is a way to pretend, imagine and project onto or into something so that we can learn faster, deeper and more creatively. Therefore, children are the fastest learners because they make play fun and engaging.

The following events, experiences and issues are the negative ones of course, because I suspect many people reading this will only want to know how to help when a child is in distress or trouble or is having a negative experience. I don't see that many clients in therapy for issues around their excessive happiness or overuse of smiling.

The next section focuses on helping you by helping children make meaning out of the events that occur or happen to them. You can understand the situation from an informed perspective and so, most important, knowing all you do now about the body and brain, you can help them understand how to regulate their distress. We are after all bodies and brains with a negative bias. Amy R really is a power to be reckoned with!

Issues that arise

Gaming addiction/disorders have already been covered as a topic that I wanted to introduce you to; however, I had not gone into the how-to-help aspect. I hope that through the earlier discussion, you were able to see that my perspective on this issue is one of considering what the impact is and for whom before 'diagnosing' someone with a disorder. In terms of how you can help a young person with their usage, as I have already said, we need to understand the motivators behind the 'overuse' or refusal to disengage. That said, when the child is screaming that they want to continue their use regardless of the consequences, we start to enter the territory of parenting and the normal 'battles of willpower' that occur. This doesn't necessarily have to be over gaming/social media and so on. So what do you do?

I am asked this question so many times by people in and out of therapy as this seems to be in the top five most asked questions relating to cyberspace, and here is my answer: the/your child is not manipulative; they are not naughty; they are trying to communicate something to you about the importance of this 'thing', this game that they so want to continue playing. You probably first noticed this behaviour in your child around toddlerhood when the "mine" behaviour started? Do you remember that battle when you wanted something they had in their hands, and they would say "mine" and not give it back (or run away with it!)? That's because it was important to them and they wanted to exert some control or power in the relationship. They were testing out their new skills of recognising they had a choice, power and what we call autonomy. They soon learn the arduous lesson of 'the parents are in charge'; that often, the choice they have is 'no choice'; and rules, boundaries and contracts are assumed to be 'the law' (or 'I am a child and get no say in this debate').

Since then, children have become accomplished at knowing what's important to them and how to create a dynamic of 'conflict connection' with you. Yes, this probably seems strange, but often children don't know how to explain themselves with words, so they show you. In terms of our earlier stories in the book, this is about the blue and red lane communication of any connection being better than none.

So, let's go through a few scenarios to give you an idea for a way to work with this issue. They look similar, and I can't account for all parenting styles and what is said, but I can talk in a generic way. Please feel free to add the voices of your child in your head as you read these or choose a child whom you know such as Bart Simpson (yes, the cartoon figure):

'Okay, Bart, time to get off your game!'
'But . . . just five more minutes, Mum'.
'No!!! Now, Bart, we have to go to school/pick up your sister/go shopping/visit Aunt Beru/eat our lunch and so on . . .'
'But, Muuuuuuuuummmmmmm'.

At this point, what parents usually report is the start of escalation and shouting resulting in threats of turning off the game or punishments about being banned from playing ever again in their life. (We do dramatise very quickly.) I know that sounds a bit excessive, but people under pressure or who are angry are not to be reasoned with. Think red lane here: unable to listen or rationalise. This includes both parent and child. So here we are: Harmony = 0, Conflict = 1 (and counting).

So, if, like a movie, we slow things right down and go back to the start, we can see that the interactions between parent and child could have been started in a different way for a different outcome. Quite simply, all it needs is an agreement or, as we say in transactional analysis, a contract. In therapy, I contract with my clients about the sessions and what they will look like. If we are to do something like painting a picture, we might contract that activity; for example we will clear up afterwards or not, but we agree to it beforehand. We can then change the contract if we both agree, for example I might say to the client, 'We agreed to this; I wonder what it would be like if we now changed it and we did this instead? What do you think, feel or say to that?' The client can now negotiate, discuss the options or perhaps stick with their original agreement, and both of us are part of this new contract.

What I do know is that when contracts, also known as boundaries or agreements, are laid down (you may call them 'ground rules', although these seem less flexible), it makes the process of negotiating and natural consequences being discussed or implemented that little bit easier when it comes to the contract being broken in any way. For example we can talk about the agreement or contract and say something like, 'Do you remember when we agreed to x, y, z and we agreed that this would happen if the contract was broken?' It's less conflictual and still manages to address the issue, and when this feels like a co-created action, people are less likely to retaliate, respond and or react with anger. Now, it doesn't mean they won't react like that, and sometimes they will, but it's much less likely.

Boundaries is a word I use to educate parents about 'rules'; now, this doesn't mean rules that are fixed and like iron fences; this is like the surface film on water (called the meniscus). You can be flexible without breaking it, or indeed, you can move the liquid to another receptacle to allow a new meniscus to form. To quote Bruce Lee, 'become the teapot'. Now I am aware that during some of my teaching and/or therapy sessions, parents and adults have been known to say to me, 'But this means the children are manipulating us and they're getting away with it and they won't respect us, and they'll walk all over us!' And here is what I respond with:

I'm not here to tell you that my parenting is the most wonderful (it certainly isn't). I have a fairly good memory of being a child and now I can see what a difficult role parenting must have been for my parents (I wasn't always a rule follower). However, put yourself in the child's shoes for just a moment. See if you can remember being a child yourself? Do you have child or teen amnesia, or can you really get in touch with how the following used to be for you?

You are having fun playing a game (any sort) and you have been asked to stop for reasons you may not have been told? (Think of the line 'because I said so' here!). How much did you respect this? How much did you really want to change the situation to carry on playing? How much did you want to stop and walk away (from the game, the computer, your friends)? Or perhaps we come right up to date and you reflect on *when you were last at a party, event or gig and were enjoying yourself. Suddenly a person (e.g. a door supervisor) came in and turned off/on the lights and music, pushed the speaker or musician off the stage and said, 'Time to go to bed or home, because I said so and that's that'. How would you feel?

*Of course, this may have been before 2020, and I am sure the lockdowns will have also felt very similar for many of us. 'Stay at home' has become a national trigger for that 'grounding' punishment and parallels the preceding so much!

Now the next part of the reflection may just get a little bit uncomfortable for a moment. So I will try to do this tongue in tongue-in-cheek to alleviate the slight frustration, anger and denial that might just pop up in you. Are we not manipulating children into doing what we want because we are the grown-ups and we are demanding what we want?

When the children don't want to do what we have asked, nagged or shouted about, we get angry and often demand compliance! Then we say stuff like 'They're manipulative', 'They're controlling' and, the one that's most often uttered in the therapy room, 'I can't let them win this one as they'll try it on every time'.

I wonder who is doing the controlling here and what game this is that adults have to win? Could parenting be a game? I wonder what your relationship with games might be: Are you a play all to win, competitive, perfectionist or sore loser? Are our children pieces in a game, or could we see our role here as similar but different?

Yes, parenting is difficult at times and, yes, we ask our children to do things and they refuse, ignore us and generally act like . . . children. Because that's exactly what they are. I'm not saying that we must pander to their wishes or agenda every time, nor do we have to negotiate on every occasion. However, what I'm suggesting is that we let the children in on the contract or ground rules we set in our heads before we begin letting them know they have broken them in some way. It's really confusing otherwise.

This means more explicit communication in the form of before giving them the gaming consoles, new games and profiles we discuss what we expect in terms of behaviour around them. This, however, is also an ongoing discussion with them, not a one-stop contract. Children are not mind-readers, and they seriously don't know what they are supposed to do if we don't tell them. Perhaps you can draw up a written contract and call it a fluid and negotiable one. Be aware this holds you accountable also. If you renegotiate about times, days and games (ratings/styles, etc.), add this to the contract.

Because you don't know in advance what games are due out soon until your children tell you or what the emerging trends will be or where gaming technology is heading, you need to be able to adapt your contract to meet the changing landscape. The gaming industry is very good at creating content that children (and adults) want to play continuously and with friends. It's the industry's job, and it is the leader and best at it.

In terms of healthy time on games, that is up to you as a family to decide, and again, what's healthy now may not be when new games are released. If your children's friends are playing it the moment it is released, this adds a bit of pressure to the mix. If you think about popular games in terms of items or toys that were trendy when you were a child; this is often a similar concept, for example Adidas trainers, Pokémon cards or Tamagotchi.

To date, the only recommendations about games exist in the world of research, where we don't have any real answers. Most forms of advice about games and time spent on them come from other parents or adults (perhaps trying to sell you a course or two?). There's plenty of advice on social media to create a feeling of uncertainty about your parenting. If your child does not do what Mrs Mumonline1984 suggests is 'normal', it can leave you feeling like you're parenting in a way that's less than perfect. This new influx of information and advice is also our cross to bear when using our own social media. It is the constant parenting advice given online based on, in most circumstances, the parenting of one or maybe four or five children at most, not a whole generation or professional factual-based research.

In my favour, and why I can talk to you about this topic in depth, is that I have been using computers and gaming since the 1980s. I was curious about my children's use of the new technology and learned about the games they played by both watching and playing them myself. (I have been overbearing and a nuisance at times with the questions apparently!) I have been privy to lots of potential issues you may now face with your children. My children are now adults in their 20s, and as such, there is a whole heap of questions that have been answered along the way. Now working with games and gamers of all ages in therapy and playing the games myself, I find questions still continue to arise and be answered. It is likely your questions will be here too.

So how do you get your child to put the game down/turn it off?

When I teach, I use the analogy of gaming as the 'spaghetti test'. How long does it take to cook spaghetti: 7, 12 or 25 minutes? Well, the answer depends on several things – the type of spaghetti, how soft you want it, whether you added it to cold or salt water and so on. And so it is with games; each type, style or 'episode' is different. Each game has a different outcome and sections when you can save your progress, leave without affecting others or being heard by them and so on. If you have this knowledge in your arsenal you can work around this and parenting around games becomes that bit easier. Game knowledge here can really help.

When approaching your child who is engaged and immersed in a/the game, my advice is to treat this situation akin to a small animal you are trying to catch unaware and to tread carefully, speak calmly and remember your prosody (tone and loudness), rather than exasperated tones or shouting. Learning about a style of communication called non-violent communication can help you request rather than demand, and I can tell you the results are striking as to how the conversation goes once you become adept at using this. You may feel this is 'liberal parenting'; however, the research supports this approach as the easiest, least conflictual approach, so maybe you can try it to see how it fits. I'm all for easy options as it leaves me with more energy to devote to the things that really matter in my life. Remember the part about challenge resulting in conflict or rebellion? I hope you can find a way that leans towards cooperation and calm because it feels so much nicer for you all.

Reflect that you can see they're having fun and learning new skills (showing them empathy and connection) and saying, 'However . . . we (making it co-created) need to do/go/be/have/get. . .' and ask where they're at in the game as this will give you the information you need for your next sentence. This is important, and you will now have the child's motivator (i.e. they must capture the flag/get to the end of this mission/ save point and so on). At this point then, you can set a time/boundary limit WITH them around the motivator. For example 'Okay, so when you hit the next save point, it's time to come off' (it helps to know what the save points look like by the way so you can check for compliance).

Here is a really important step so you both know where you stand; ask the child to repeat the boundary back to you verbally. A child who has listened can do exactly this. If they cannot, rinse and repeat. You may also potentially be labelled as putting them off or interrupting, nagging, being annoying or doing it on purpose here. If this is the case, it's not personal; it is because they are finding it distracting. (We all have an experience of this trying to read something and a person starts asking us questions. Remember your empathy.)

Also, a helpful piece of advice is don't ask the child to come off the game at the exact moment you want them to (i.e. 'NOW'); give warnings in advance; it really does help. For example 'We need to leave in 10 minutes so the game needs to be turned off in 5 minutes so you can get yourself ready in time'.

Hint: Perhaps get yourself a kitchen timer and set it behind the child (rather than in front as they may change the timer or alarm on it, I know would!) and let them know that when it rings, they will be expected to turn it off. The word *expect* is a communication to them about their compliance. (Point of note, when typing these words, I went way beyond the time I had given myself for writing, including ignoring the timer I set. It's easily done, and my reflection here is we can all fall foul to being in the moment).

When it results in a battle, argument or flare-up

If there is a time they overshoot, deny or ignore the contract and you now find yourself reminding them of their non-compliance, which they likely hear as 'failure', be aware that this feels shameful, and reactions are likely (many parents do this without thinking because they are stressed and feeling like they have been ignored). Your child decided to continue past the boundary point for all the reasons we have and will discuss, and now they're probably feeling guilty or angry. There will also be times they have pushed the boundary to wind you up because they could or because they don't care.

Your job here as the adult is to wait till the pair of you are both back 'on-line' (calm) to have a discussion and repair the moment. This is a way to build respect between you both and gives you both an opportunity to reflect and consider the contract, boundary or rules and perhaps make some slight alterations in favour of what you consider healthy for your family. Sounds easy, doesn't it? I do know these moments first-hand, and I like you had to learn how to approach this with many 'repairs' along the way. I know that compared to my friends and family, I didn't have as many 'flare-ups' with my children regarding games because I played them and I remembered being a child myself. It sucks to not be in a place of power and control.

To give you a little insight into two issues in gaming and how parents can miss the importance behind the issues, I'm going to talk about save points 'saves' and not having to watch campaign or story videos – 'video skips' – and how this affected one young person.

A young boy had played a very popular adventure game called Zelda on a hand console. He had accrued about 3,000 hours of playtime over several many months. This meant playing the game, watching the introductory and campaign story videos to each section (which you cannot skip on the first play of the game), solving puzzles and gaining points, treasures and exchangeable items for later in the game. This was the pride and joy of this boy as he struggled with a parent who was bedridden with a terminal illness, so he would play the game in the chair at the side of the bed whilst she slept. He was further into the game than his peers, so he could help them and discussed this at school with them, and he was able to engage with his peers socially. One afternoon whilst he was at a friend's dad gave the hand console to his nephew. The child's cousin (age 7) deleted the game file (3,000 hours of playtime) and started a new game for himself.

All the client's game history, hours and achievements lost. Forever. I bet you can understand why this child was outraged and angry and cried for days. I'm sure you can understand that when he came to me in therapy, brought for 'gaming addiction', I did not see this as a gaming disorder but as a child who was in pain and hurting. His dedication to his game was as a tool to manage his distress; he was in pain about his mother's terminal illness and the deletion of his game. This wasn't just the physical loss but that of the feeling of betrayal by the parent who didn't understand the deletion of this save (it came to light in further sessions that the cousin may well have known exactly what this would do and may well have been sabotage). He was also seriously irked at having to watch all the videos again as part of his gameplay. His parents at the time did not understand this commitment or the gameplay issues and had said to him, that he was overreacting and to 'just play it again; it can't be that bad'.

I wonder if they had understood the gameplay and time and effort that had been lost or known about the videos having to be watched all over again whether they would have discounted or dismissed the reaction of the child so? Do you remember the example of the Lego tower? Have you ever suffered the time spent dedicated to a project and it was lost somehow? Students often suffer this with corrupt files, lost flash drives or essays, and it has the same impact and emotional outbursts. Loss hurts.

References

Brown, S., & Vaughn, C. (2009). *Play. How it shapes the brain, opens the imagination and invigorates the soul*. Penguin Avery.

Cozolino, L. (2006). *The neuroscience of human relationships: Attachment and the developing social brain* (1st ed.). WW Norton & Co.

9 Gaming issues, risks and pitfalls

Introduction
The risks or pitfalls

This is generally the main topic of conversation anywhere I look nowadays, which brings me to the introduction of gaming-related issues – not disorders here but the potential for things to occur when playing games. Before I begin to use terminology here, I'm going to re-introduce the concepts. Gaming behaviour is about fun and relationships within or to the game. No man is an island as they say. So the same goes for children and young people playing games. Motivations need to be understood in the context of relationships. And games are the arena in which relationships, skills and achievements are found or developed.

Leaving games

First, we looked at the not wanting to leave the game when asked to by a parent. However, leaving the game also comes under relationships in terms of children wanting to stay and play because of the following:

1. They are having a great time/fun.
2. They want to please their friends by continuing to collaborate and win games, levels or campaigns and so on.
3. They want to play to impress their friends with their gaming skills.
4. They want to be the last one to leave (think about the people who leave the parties last).
5. They want to gain more experience points so they can show off (be ahead of the crowd).
6. They want to beat or master a challenge. For me, it was 'that darn scarab beetle' so I could tell and show my children I had done it. This can help 'unlock' levels, points and rewards or is just satisfying to complete (after failing so many times, well, in my case anyway).

DOI: 10.4324/9781003169390-11

7   The quality of the game designed has saves that are far apart in terms of time, points or distance in the game.

8   They don't want to engage with family members.

9   They use it as escapism from abuse, where this virtual space feels safer.

10   Abuse is occurring, and the threat of leaving is deemed too great.

11   Romance and wanting to spend time with their partner, or to create a romantic relationship with a new partner (by having the same interests/hobbies/games).

12   They want to wind their parents/family members up in terms of deliberately staying on.

13   They want to destroy someone else's progress.

14   They're in flow/the zone.

15   They want to gain points to buy things for the game that could (a) display their skill level as part of their online identity, (b) allow them to upgrade a weapon/technique/skill that is only available to a particular class/level and (c) display the latest skin/**avatar** and show this off (this is a little like Experience points (**XP points**) but is a highly visual character upgrade, whereas XP points is a point system that people can see and may not be as obvious deeding upon the platform and console).

When you ask your child to come off the game, how would you know which one of the 15 reasons is the one they are protesting about? (There's probably a lot more than 15 to be honest.)

What can we do as parents and professionals?

First, we need to ascertain the motivation and connect with the underlying feelings and thoughts of the child in order to work with the previously mentioned issues. We can choose to limit, remove, ban, coerce away from and beg or plead; however, the factor I have found most helpful for parents when discussing this issue is like the one discussed earlier, and this is to learn about the games, learn about the consequences of leaving the game early and work with your child around this.

Not only does this help you communicate with your child about their gaming experience, but it also strengthens an attachment-based feeling in the child as they often feel important when a parent takes an interest in their experience. I am not saying we must 'give into' the child's demands of staying on games or for them never turning them off. However, you can see with the 15 reasons they are often complicated and perhaps ones that adults hadn't considered.

And as discussed with one parent in therapy about the child not leaving the game for dinner, the natural consequence would be cold food which invariably teaches its own lesson (spaghetti Bolognese is really icky when it's cold). Sometimes as parents we can choose to 'get into a battle', or we can perhaps let things run naturally as in the dinner example, or we can put the boundaries in place before the event, for example no gaming before dinner, eliminating most of the difficulties.

I'm aware this is not always easy, and sometimes this is where we can have our flexible contract in terms of trying out gaming before dinner: If the child is late to the table, then the contract states that they would not be able to game before dinner for x number of days. This resembles adult life for example in terms of credit and loans, whereby if you are late with payments, you cannot take out further credit unit you satisfy the contract you have with the creditor – life lessons in a manageable and age-appropriate way.

I'm aware that sometimes, some parents use the games as a way to keep children busy whilst they prepare dinner or tend to online meeting or emails, and then they face the issues above because the contract wasn't discussed or even understood. This is when we cannot have our cake and eat it if we want to have a balanced relationship with games and our family life.

Communication, communication, communication.

Kicking/pushing from games

This is where others 'kick' or 'push' you out of a game. This is rejection, bullying, abuse, unfair and debilitating at times. It's also banter and teasing. How do children or young people know the difference and what is the impact? This behaviour happens in the real world, but online, it can be subtler or indeed far more obvious. So why would someone else kick/push you from a game? Fun? Silliness or bullying? Again, there're lots of reasons. I've spoken with children in therapy who talk about why they kick/push and with those who have been kicked/pushed.

To cover why children kick/push they have given the following reasons:

> [I]t's bantz (banter), for the lols (a laugh), I wanted the points, the player was shit, too many head shots, not enough of x behaviour (e.g. reviving, supporting, following), the player was deliberately camping out (staying in one spot), the player was talking all the time or sending excessive chats, stole my treasure/prize/health/pack etc, the player was a kid, the player was an adult, the player was a 'weirdo' or

'pedo' (young people use this word a lot, with no evidence and use it as a slur rather than concerned actual worry; more on this later), the player was too good, the player set me up, the player destroyed something of mine, we don't like him/her/them, it was a joke, they were a liberty, they can't play, they're English/American/Portuguese and all other racist comments. They're a girl/boy or other gender or sexuality. We did it in secret (group chat) and we did it publicly.

Pretty much sounds like when children are playing games like hide-and-seek, football, or tig to name a few outdoor games? This sounds like human behaviour, period. Yet in a computer game what are the rules and norms?

Why children who have been kicked/pushed think/reason/believe they were kicked/pushed:

I'm rubbish, they hate me, I can't play, I only said a joke, in English/ Welsh/Chinese, I'm small, I'm tall, I'm fat, I'm skinny, and all other manner of issues that begin with 'I AM'.

Again, these sound like the reasons a child might give when teachers/ parents or other people ask why the child is 'upset' about the game. When the child reveals what has happened or why they are feeling sad rejected, lonely and other emotional responses. Adults can sometimes not understand the response or the importance of the game. I wonder if you heard phrases such as 'it's only a game' or 'there're only playing' when you experienced something like this in real life as a child.

All emotions shown highlight how distressed a child may be when they are deliberately pushed out of a game by others, and often this is interpreted as a personal attack resulting in a feeling of unworthiness. To highlight this, some studies were conducted that involved people, adults, playing a computer game whilst having their brain activity monitored in a functional magnetic resonance imaging machine. The players thought they were playing the game with other humans but were playing against a computer. They would randomly be ignored or pushed out of the game. When the researchers watched the brain activity, it showed that the area of physical injury and pain lit up even in this virtual scenario. The conclusion was the brain is unable to tell the difference between a virtual kick and a corporeal one, for example to the shins. We will come to this in more detail later. What this means for the children and young people playing these games is they are likely be emotionally hurt and perceive this rejection in the same way as the adults in the above research. When they are kicked, it will feel like 'ouch', and we know from real-life situations, rejection in young people is often accompanied by expressions of those emotions; that is they may shout, cry and stamp their feet.

In terms of attachment-based responses and reactions to this kicking/ pushing, children may have certain behaviours and enduring times for those responses: securely attached children may be hurt for a while, and with the help of an adult or other person, they may work through this quickly and respond with a resilient approach to playing once more. It won't be long before a securely attached child can 'trust' once more.

Avoidant attachment may result in the child deciding they don't want to play the game again (they may say ever again!) and they may refuse to play the game or stay away from it for some time. Or they may choose to keep swapping games to avoid continuous rejections. It may take them some time to trust others in games.

Ambivalent attachment may result in a 'I don't care' reaction, yet they will want to play on the game, followed by angry outburst toward the game or players of it. They don't want to miss playing it and really don't want to play it. They may find excuses to play and, of course, react by doing this to others in a hurt them before they hurt you approach.

Disorganised attachments will be a mixture of all these responses with no apparent pattern. For children with attachment issues such as children in foster care, adoption or care homes, these outbursts may be exaggerated and is tied into their inner feelings of 'not being wanted/good enough' before they even turn the console on, let alone play the game and get pushed/kicked and have this amplified.

What can we do as parents/carers/professionals?

We can attempt to attune and empathise with the rejection, remembering what this felt like for us. For example when you were at school during physical activities, were you not picked, picked last, cheated, ignored or pushed around in some way during a game? This is the same sort of thing, only perhaps in the child's experience, this feels a much bigger deal due to the bigger 'audience'.

We can avoid saying, when possible, 'it's just a game' or 'don't be silly' because for the child, it's not 'just' a game, nor are their feelings and reactions silly; they are what they are based on how the child feels in that moment. We can reflect that we understand how tough it is, how these moments suck and how you will support them in their decision to play versus not play the game again. Children need support and choice and to have someone be there no matter what. I can tell you that in my practice, one of the most reported feelings for children and young people is the parent 'being too busy to notice their pain' or 'rejecting' or 'dismissing it' which, as discussed, is as painful as a physical rejection, and this is coming from a parent so may well have more 'ouch' to it.

I have no doubt one of the most difficult feelings for us to manage is rejection and isolation. It's why the lockdown was and is a big issue for many people.

During the game: destruction/sabotage

I'm sure that for most of you reading this book, you will have seen computer games that involve collecting things, building things and doing things (alone or together) as the main purpose of the game (pretty much sums up most games I suppose). Gone are the days of just 'levelling up' as in Pac-Man/Space Invaders and attempting to be on a leader board at the local arcade.

I am talking here about games that increase a player's experience points or rewards for completion of tasks known as Achievements. This is usually a viewable score that other players can see attached to your gamertag (name on the console/game) along with trophies, badges or levels such as 'Prestige'. A little bit like the letters after your name: Dr, Dame or Professor.

Games that children play that involve building something like a village in Minecraft (still popular, but by the time this book is out this may have changed again) or team games in which capturing the flag or reconnaissance point is the aim of the game. So why sabotage? Well, we're back to the Lego tower for a moment. This is where other players will deliberately sabotage the aim/end point of a game for the 'lols' (what is commonly known as having a laugh at the expense of another). This is when for example an 8-year-old has mined and built a castle, spent ages designing the contents of the castle and grounds and along comes another player and ruins it (e.g. by setting it on fire or letting sheep or cats loose – I know, don't ask!). Anyway, the result is that all the child's hard work – destroyed in one fell swoop. Or, in the case of some games, players are playing and just as they are about to capture the flag, a number of the players or the host suddenly leaves, meaning the game is over and the server cuts them off it (rather like earlier with kicking). The result of this can be a loss of achievements or XP points and a whole heap of frustration.

How does this happen? Usually, this occurs when a child invites one of their friends (another gamer) to their village, server or party (or perhaps it's hacked and a player gets into it; although rare, it is possible). This can happen whilst the child is playing the game or as I have seen with a client playing Minecraft, whilst they are away from their console (i.e. asleep), and they return to the destruction of the village (this sounds a little bit like Vikings, doesn't it?). The distress for the child is because they know the saboteur or because they do not know who did this or why. It can also happen with saves where another person accidentally or deliberately deletes the saved information (as in the story from earlier). Why does this happen? Pretty much for the same reason anyone who decided they can hurt another person for a laugh: because they can or because they enjoy hurting others. These saboteurs may not be children either.

The result is mostly sadness, confusion, anger ranging from frustration to rage, disappointment, betrayal and many more emotions. In terms of attachment, this behaviour can lead a secure child to temporarily feel rejected/abandoned; however, they are fairly resilient in terms of knowing they can 'build it back up' or 'play another game'. However, in terms of insecure attachment (all three styles), this really does feel more permanent and taps into the feelings of uselessness, unworthiness, rejection, abandonment and/or feeling unwanted or betrayed, and this can result in loss of trust. This is really difficult for them to manage.

What can we do as parents/carers/professionals?

We can initially contain the child's frustration as we would do if a child's Lego tower fell or their 'airfix model' broke after hours of gluing and sticking. We can avoid schadenfreude when possible; this is when we laugh at another's misfortune, a bit like the popular TV programme *Have You Been Framed*. We can offer our sympathy and empathy about having all the hard work and effort sabotaged by another person. This really is a place of pain for these children.

Have you ever been writing something on a computer and forgot to click the save button and the computer died or blue-screened you (the screen goes blue, hence the name) and all your work was lost. Imagine someone did this to you deliberately. How would you feel? It's pretty much that feeling your child is experiencing. Distressing, isn't it? Would you want or seek revenge? Would you talk about it incessantly until you feel better? This occupied talking about the event is how many of us manage our stress, disappointment, anger, frustrations and so on. It helps us feel better, so ask your child to talk about what has happened and listen in carefully for their pain so you can help them manage it.

Bugging/camping out and other 'unfair' #cheats? #headshots

This is when, during the game, one player has a 'sweet spot' that allows them to ambush/catch others out time and time again. Unfair headshots are when the player scopes in on you (zooms in) from a distance and has an advantage for shooting and killing, and you have no idea where they are. This is akin to a sniper's role and is mostly applicable to FPS games. I'm not sure if you have ever carried out behaviour like this. I have, particularly when playing laser quest against my colleagues and definitely in the 'ambush' elements of live-firing training in the military. I also might have hidden behind a door or two on unsuspecting friends and family members.

Why does this happen? I can only summarise this as a behaviour that, in its own right, is meant to prevent the player (cheater) from losing because maybe they are afraid to, are sore losers, need to win, must win. Losing feels terrible to them. Why would you play fair if you could find a way that meant you didn't have to? Perhaps they may have an insecure attachment or emotional regulation difficulty or a learning disability and would struggle to lose or know the 'rules of the game' of fair play and socialising.

What results from this behaviour is a feeling of unjustness and unfairness for the other players, and this can be one of the most prominent reasons for kicking/pushing or reporting players. It really is a big deal to both the person camping out and those who do not. Why does this really happen? Well, this is slightly more complicated than 'just hiding'. This kind of behaviour results from the experiences a child has within their families and friendship circles. If we look at families for example a child who has to 'be perfect' for their parents to avoid chastisement will always look for ways to 'prove' this perfectness. This may mean playing more on a game to become so perfect or in this case; cheating so they can say, 'Look I'm the best/top of the class', and in turn, this means the child receives their parent's care/attention and love. However, this consistently becomes an unachievable outcome for the child. The seeking behaviour results in escalations of what it takes to be the best and of course in gaming this presents itself as this kind of behaviour. The self-worth of the child is based on the outcomes of their behaviours rather than on being loved unconditionally with all their flaws. So, when I say the child who can't lose really can't because, if they did, they may encounter an angry parent who criticises or punishes, it's in their interest to win at all costs.

However, if they are then kicked from the game for cheating, they will feel further rejection, this taps into the feelings of not being perfect, and they will cheat more in order to win. Their anger or trying-hard attitude covers the feelings of rejection and loss of perceived love. Children in therapy often say 'they can't win' so they might as well cheat as they have nothing to lose and all to gain in terms of admiration from their parents and peers for winning. This is why children carry out this behaviour in the real world too. It's a projection of needing to feel wanted, important, special and accepted.

What can we do as parents/carers/professionals?

We can create a world that is both competitive and understanding to the losers as well as the winners. By this I mean, my children grew up in time when disappointment was negated and discounted within their primary school. All activities were equal and fair, and there were no outright winners. It was all about the taking part, and whilst this is a valid viewpoint for 'fairness', it is not equality or true to the skills a child needs to become resilient (hence, I took them to sports clubs because they replicate real life).

This 'all's equal' is not how life is, and it resulted in a cohort of children who are now ages 18 to 26-ish that have been labelled by the media as snowflakes and having an assumption that they are 'entitled'. Which, is a fair assumption based on a history of win or lose you will get a reward to be celebrated?

If a child does not understand the feeling of disappointment through loss and is not supported to manage this, how do they learn to be humble in victory? Perhaps they don't, and they bug out in a game, taking hedonic pleasure in winning. It's no wonder those who understand loss feel cheated is it? We as adults can help children learn to deal with loss in its many forms and to support our children through the painful feelings associated with it. In terms of the attachment theory I've introduced you to, this feeling of losing is the deep fear we all fear and comes from the social rejection we would face if we did not 'win' the food for our family or we lost our way in the tribe. This is deep-rooted (you could say in our DNA) and is why it is so darn difficult for young children to manage; it's a feeling they do not understand. Sometimes, I'm not sure adults do too.

Other issues that cause frustration: lagging, glitches and processors

So you bought your children a console and set it up connecting all the wires and connecting to the network (ethernet or Wi-Fi), and hey, presto, your child is ready to go. They sign into their new game, connect with their friends and begin the new trendy game of the day/week/month/year. And then it all goes pear-shaped because just as they are about to, then they all laughed until their stomachs hurt.

The end.

Frustrating, isn't it! Don't you just want to know what happened in the story, and did you do a double take on the text? Did you feel like the sentence had not been printed properly? It's almost like some words in this book fell out onto the floor and now you'll never know what happened in between. Does this sound familiar? How do you react as an adult when the film or music pauses then jumps to the next part, or there's a glitch in the technology when you're trying to present or teach (just me then?), or when you have been watching a TV programme, the phone or door rings and by answering it you miss the main part? (Although in today's world, this doesn't happen much thanks to the live-TV pause button, and of course, you can rewind too).

Without getting technical, I will simplify the next few parts of the explanation with easy-to-understand concepts. I will skip over talking about frames per second on monitors, which is a very important aspect of this issue and is one that can only really be fixed by buying good monitors (or having a very good technical know-how with settings). In the world of gaming, it is really important to have two important factors: a fast processor in the gaming device/computer and a fast internet connection that allows the gameplay to refresh and stay 'in the race' with the other players. I address the internet connection first as the last point as this leads to the console/PC issue.

So many children can get annoyed and frustrated when their internet connection is the tortoise compared to their friend's superfast broadband hare. This may be an issue with the provider and the type of connection (e.g. Wi-Fi is slower than hard-line connections) and could just be that lots of people in the house, street or country are connected all at the same time. This may also be an issue in which financial and socio-economic status have an impact. For example, if Joe is upper class and can afford the latest and fastest broadband, his connection will be more stable and allow for faster streaming and gaming compared to Adam, who might only be able to afford the small Wi-Fi box in the house that came as part of a phone deal. The way these two players would be able to connect to and maintain that solid connection throughout the game would be very different. It is highly likely, and often happens, that one player remains connected throughout the game and the other players internet connection keeps dropping off or is so slow that they jump through the game in sections rather than a fluid story. This is the frustration of trying to 'game when the connection is poor'. Think of lagging behind when you're trying to walk with the children and they can't keep up with you. It can feel like you walk twice the distance (doubling back or slowing down to be alongside them).

Now if this social class or economic status is anything to consider as a problem for gaming then you have the Joneses up front. Some children will consistently beg for the latest console when it is announced because children understand that the latest console (e.g. PS5, Xbox S) will have better processing speeds and the ability to produce better graphics which means the games will require more processing power to run smoothly.

And they want it for a number of reasons: first, to play alongside their peers and not be left out and, second, because it's new. (Brains like new and novel things, which is why you likely have a lot of stuff that's better than the one before right?) Marketers know this, and this is why popular brands of washing powder are 'the best yet' and 'get whites whiter than any product ever before'. (I wonder if this is actually possible; I mean how white can white be?). And of course, they are marketed to sell a month before Christmas to ensure 'pester power' creates those sales and the game sales for them too.

If for example one child's parents can only afford the original Xbox, then they will not be able to play up-to-date games because their console 'cannot handle it'. This will become a known fact with their peers when they are unable to join them on the games. Furthermore, it is often the case that children display their console preferences in discussions with each other, and it is part of their gaming 'peer profile' (not gamertag), rather like the designer clothing people wear. The issue here is this is like children playing sports where the affluent family has 'all the gear'. Other poorer children can only ask to borrow it or buy fakes. Moreover, this has been a regular contributing factor, children tell me in the therapy room, as to why they avoid playing games online because 'my friends will know I'm poor, because I only have a. . . (console/device)' or 'I pretend I don't like the game, so no one knows'.

What can we do as parents/professionals?

Understanding how the aspect of lagging leads to frustration is fairly easy for us to see and work with. We simply connect with the frustration of being interrupted ourselves. As for consoles, Well (sarcasm inbound here), we could keep buying into the consumerism bubble of having the latest device/console/computer/TV and so on and be so broke that we cannot feed or clothe our children properly anymore but have no fear they could photoshop designer clothes and Michelin-star food into their photos!

Or, on a serious note, perhaps we can be realistic and take notice of the socio-economic aspect of owning technology and how families need to find a way to manage this distress with their child. We cannot stop the competitive nature of the console wars, the console game elitism (whereby games only appear for one console), and we could look at why children are finding friendships so difficult to manage in a world in which keeping up with the Joneses may well be resulting in poverty in families who see technology as a necessity, which, of course, became essential during the lockdowns of 2020. I wonder if this dug the hole a little deeper for some families. Social equality is certainly not fair in 2020.

This is where we as parents can step in and connect with our child and recognise these feelings and reflect that we too feel like this at times in the world (envy), and we also know how it feels when things are not fair and equal. We do not have to explain in detail to our children that we cannot afford everything (they take this on as a responsibility to not spend your money). Neither do we need to attack the child's parents who can afford and buy these things. We can help our children manage this through empathic attunement.

In terms of attachment theory, securely attached children are able to manage the disappointments slightly easier than insecurely attached children regarding owning the latest console or game or managing their distress tolerance of glitches and lagging, although any person who is being constantly interrupted does find at times their patience is tested, and this is normative to find yourself sometimes erring on the side of impatience and 'percussive maintenance' also known as bashing the device (gently, of course!).

10 Abuse in gaming

From bullying to exploitation

Introduction

Abuse is a rather broad definition of various acts set to cause harm and distress. Abuse can be physical, mental or emotional and, in gaming, can follow any one of these paths or all of them together. I will briefly explain each one of these, including how they impact a child. The examples here are ones that are both intentionally carried out by one or more persons on one or more recipients and those that are unintentional. I believe this point is very important as we often see reported the intentional act of abuse, and yet human beings are not always that aware of our impact on another person when we ourselves are 'in our own heads' or lacking empathy and consideration for others in that moment.

Humans are mostly good-willed and kind, and because we are human, we are prone to carrying out behaviours that are not intended to cause alarm, distress, upset or offence but often do. As I said earlier, much of the narrative and literature surrounding digital or technology-related issues is pathologising and labelling and omits the fact we are humans with intentions that can, unknowingly, cause distress. This does not make it okay that we engage in behaviour that hurts another person, nor do the following reasons mean that we can behave in this way and 'blame' our personality or anything else that we feel may get us off the hook.

First, in the area to discuss, there is name-calling as a direct form of abuse which may constitute bullying or in the realm of online/internet related or cyberspace this tends to be called 'cyberbullying'. This definition is contested and difficult to pin down because it overlaps so many other variants and types of behaviour, and of course, it often accompanies real-world abuse at the same time. I have a definition that describes this behaviour, and it is similar to the definition of cybertrauma and includes one-time events, which many if not all the current definitions do not.

DOI: 10.4324/9781003169390-12

This is because in cyberspace, the power dynamic and repetition referred to in many of the standard bullying definitions does not need to be present as the 'perpetrator', in this case, may not have a power differential that we see in the real world (of course, being a bully is often about power) one-time events can be permanent, and of course, this may not even be a person perpetrator but a machine learning algorithm (see my definition of *cybertrauma* on my website http://www.childrenandtech. co.uk). Notwithstanding, it is very rarely a one-time event that someone is abused in this way, but it might just be this one time, on this one game, for this one child.

This next discussion infers that sound is available via speakers and, in some parts, that the microphone of the gamer(s) is switched on.

Name-calling in gaming

Name-calling can often be about many things ranging from a critique of your gaming ability or lack of it. The number of XP points you have or don't have, your avatar, gamertag, team name, age, location, voice, a lack of voice, lagging issues, the console you're using, the version of a game you have or don't have, the games that you have played, are a fan of, the choices you make within games, understanding of a game, whether your parents call you off games, your spelling in the chat logs, your acronyms, your weapons of choice, your car colour, games you fear, console rivalry and whether you have the latest gadgets for each console. The names can also be about your race, religion, family status, class, finances, intelligence, age, sex, gender, sexuality and, in certain cases, any information that people can 'find' about you such as criminal convictions or social media posts.

This name-calling can be carried out by one or multiple persons online and can result in 'tag teams' or 'gangs' (cybermobs) of abusers targeting one player. It can be audio in the forms of shouting during a game, voice messages to the players inbox or visual during the game or to the inbox (during or after games). It can also be in levels of 'adult language' and swearing. It can be aggressive and threatening, malicious, vitriolic and rather mundane all at the same time from varying numbers of players.

Why and when does this happen?

Often, it's frustration from players who want their team to win. It can be purposeful. It can be jovial. It can be intended to be motivational. It can be ignorance. It can be because a person who lacks social skills and appropriate conduct skills; it can be emotional dysregulation. It can be anger.

It can be vengeful. It generally results in the recipient feeling rejected, useless, unwanted, mocked or hated. Mostly, it leaves the recipient hurt and distressed.

In terms of brains and their ability to distinguish corporeal and virtual, this would be akin to a child playing football and the other team members or spectators hurling verbal abuse at a child. Remarkably, we do not allow this on grass-roots football or rugby (although it still occurs). Crowd behaviour often contains the behaviours above and can be contagious for field sports or gaming (think of the professional versions and the crowds here).

Why this occurs may also be a connection seeking behaviour of a child. I am not saying that all children will engage in behaviour that results in abuse but bear with me whilst I explain that some children may actively look towards creating this dynamic in online gaming. This is where attachment theory can really help us understand the motivation of a child's behaviour and the meaning that underlies this. The intention of creating an environment to actively receive abuse is always based on attachment patterns and the way that transactions of love, care and attention needed happen within the family of that child.

So, to give a brief teaching on a technique I use in therapy, we can offer people in relationships 'warm fuzzies' or 'cold pricklies' (read more in Section III), which are like compliments and criticism. One feels nice, and the other, not so. However, some children thrive on the attention they receive as being negative because in an avoidant, ambivalent or disorganised family the dynamic is often 'any attention is better than none'. They will seek out this kind of abuse and grab 'cold pricklies' and reject 'warm fuzzies'.

This reinforces several things for the child which may be that they are indeed 'horrid', 'bad' or 'unwanted' with a side of 'but at least I'm noticed by them/that person'. In terms of brain development, nervous system regulation and connection, this kind of behaviour provides them with a form of connection, albeit not so great. Traumatised children or those with attachment issues often seek this behaviour out in the real world, and this is much easier to evoke online.

What can we do as parents and professionals?

This is not an attack on or a lecture about your parenting. Do not dismiss the impact or meaning the name-calling has on a child as you are not them and do not know how this feels to be them. You can guess, you can assume, and you can intuit, but you cannot know for sure as you are not in their head. And of course, you may not know the full context or history behind the name-calling at this point. Listen to hear.

What seems innocent language is not always received in this way. How did it feel when I started the paragraph with the words *do not*? Did you feel defensive because you know your child and don't 'want' or 'need' advice from some do-gooder? Language can create feelings in us before we are aware of what is happening, and name-calling can be particularly cutting and hurtful. These are the child's feelings, and they are valid. Period. They are like pins and needles: they happen, you cannot just make them go away and they can be annoying. They take up space in your attention and like a hungry caterpillar they want more attention. Munch, munch, munch!

We can empathise, model and say, 'I remember when. . .' and recall when someone called us a name. We show that we understand these feelings, but it is not a competition, and we do not have to, in the words of my 7 year old client; 'find a name that was 'worserer than theirs' (a direct quote about what his brother does). We are aiming for empathy, not victory.

The brain, as I have said, cannot distinguish between a physical attack or belief (what it thinks), so the old rhyme of 'sticks and stones hurting but words do not' has actual neuroscientific support of it being a rubbish rhyme. Words do hurt.

We can as the adults listen and help the child interpret the meaning, perhaps look towards the other persons' behaviour (not the persons themselves) and create a narrative that reflects attunement to the distress, acceptance of this distress and, when necessary, choosing to help them report, block and mute the other players through the power of autonomy and agency (they the child decides, and we support their decision).

We can also reflect to the child that it is not okay for this level of abuse or name-calling and that you understand how this can result in feelings of anger and/or revenge-seeking. However, if you can provide a space to reflect that it's normal to feel this way with empathy, you give your child experiences and tools to manage their emotions and regulate their responses as they grow.

Is it LOLs, LELs, bantz or 'for shits and gigs'?

I'm aware that shits and gigs is a charming and descriptive phrase, and I often do remark that I have never laughed or giggled that much, not for the latter part of that phrase. However, this is an internet meme (phrase, trend and now imagery), reflecting people having fun and under the guise of 'teasing', not bullying. The difference between banter and bullying or abuse is one I have covered in a blog (Knibbs, 2016), so I decided to explain some of that here for the purposes of ease and to highlight the difficulties in delineating the two. *Banter* means to have fun but not for the purposes of causing harm or upset directly. It is often used by people in the Armed Forces or Emergency Services to cope with the horrible situation they find themselves in. For example, cleaning out the 'latrines' in freezing cold weather, when it's pouring with rain, in gale-force winds and you haven't eaten for hours and hours. Jokes here are about keeping morale up, often are about the situation and are a well-worn and oiled part of life in these job roles.

Shits and gigs has the same overtone but is the more modern version of *bantz*. This often gets used as an after-the-fact statement, possibly when a child or the recipient shows distress at the incident or event. It can also be used as the 'reason' to engage in behaviour, and I hear this mostly from young people (not young children) as a way to 'wind up' adults, which is a super-interesting way to explain in the therapy room as create a situation and film it.

Why does this happen?

The reason people use the word *banter* or *bantz* is that it allows them to potentially be mean, bully or abusive and use this word to dismiss the behaviour under the pretence of joking. This can feel more insidious to a recipient if they perceive that the bully is 'lying' about their intention.

What can we do as parents and professionals?

With all bullying advice, there are consistencies around online safety, blocking and reporting. However, during research I conducted with counsellors and victims of several types of bullying, it became clear that validation and hearing the concerns and feelings of the victim were far more important than the advice given about safety and pragmatic solutions. Now whilst these are very important and needed, I am going to look towards what we need to do as parents and professionals. I do know that the impact of bullying can be long lasting because I work with adults in their 50s and 70s who still feel impacted by events that happened to them in primary school or when they were children and young people.

The most common response from parents comes from a well-meaning place; however, what the young person really desired more than anything was acceptance for their feelings no matter what. My advice would be to slow down with our natural responses of anger, revenge, rejection, hate and all those 'hot, fast and potentially negative' emotions that arise in us when our child has been hurt.

We can be aware of our 'dismissive' and 'can't be bothered with this again' feelings that can occur. (These lines are often said to me in my practice about children who continually 'moan' or 'whinge' about an event or has this happen often). What is felt by children who have been bullied is an attack on their very essence in the world and who they may be, want to be, think they are and not, and it is pernicious and toxic and, to use a metaphor, can be felt all the way down to their bones.

Attachment styles may well be coming clearer for you as we move through some of the issues in this section as a securely attached child is able to move past the hurt and see the intentions of another as less toxic than a child with an insecure attachment. Similarly, our interpretation of what is silly or daft may well be rooted in our history or attachment style.

Hearing your child's pain can be like a tuning fork that 'rubber bands' (snaps) you back to your childhood. If you didn't get your needs met when you were called a name, you may feel confused as to how to do this for your child or resentment about it. If you haven't worked through your pain, it can take you back into it very quickly. It's tough work, and we don't always get it spot on. Using the techniques discussed takes practice.

Exploitation or desperation?

The word exploitation usually conjures up the issue of sexual exploitation as this is the term most used in the media, and interestingly I find this word to be the most palatable way of talking about child sexual abuse in the media. The horror of this issue is too much to bear for many of us, and so language here has done a great injustice to the issue.

However, I am looking here at the term to denote several issues the child may be subjected to in respect of how others in the gaming world may 'use' another person for some form of gain, usually under coercive force (money/sex/grooming/XP points/kicking). To understand coercive force, it needs to be clarified in the context of preplanned manipulative behaviour (requiring a cognitive and thinking brain) versus repeated need-seeking behaviour (begging, pleading and consistent requests) driven by attachment behaviour. Once more, I am suggesting we need to understand the modus operandi of the perpetrator as one that is mostly driven by early childhood experiences, although not always exclusively.

This behaviour can be intentional for example to get a child to give away points or to help them kick another player. However, it can also be about desperation and longing to be in a relationship with another human being. Begging can be a last-ditch attempt due to a lack of skills around being able to connect with another person or able to manage rejection. Think of toddlers who are struggling with their emotions and tell you they "neeeeeedd" the teddy, dummy, toy and so on or the 'pester power' I talked to earlier. Again, this brings us back to connection and attachment styles and needs. Coercive behaviour is unlikely under the age of approximately 12 years of age, without a rational/cognitive link between intended outcomes and complex abstract thinking. It is more likely to be a need-seeking behaviour. This also does not mean that in those over the age 12, this kind of behaviour is only coercive. Conversations would need to be had to establish this.

As I said earlier, humans use technology and consoles; as this involves playing games on them, it is the most popular form of interaction on a device or console, and to date, this is the most prevalent form of entertainment and time structure in the world. The aspects of human behaviour that appear here and are the most concerning for my client base and children who play online games is when a person (usually an older adolescent/adult) coerces another through a form of manipulation and or blackmail to force another person to do something they may not otherwise choose to do willingly. This can also be known as peer pressure when the ages of the players are similar, if you think about how you might have been cajoled into 'doing' something as a child (like stealing sweets or playing hooky).

Why does this happen?

Is this coercion to bully or steal? Could this be peer pressure to engage in anti-connectedness, which is often called anti-social behaviour. This anti- connectedness can appear for example, as abuse through words or actions such as kicking. Here a child is persuaded by friends (who may be real-world friends or online friends) to abuse/kick another player. They might be messaged privately to do this or part of a group chat and called for example a yellow belly if they don't join the 'us' or 'our team' (the in-group). This peer pressure results in behaviours that are abusive/unkind and bullying to other children. The child may feel uncomfortable engaging with this behaviour but does so to relieve themselves of the pressure from others to avoid rejection or meanness happening to them.

This may also happen to a child if other players have previously heard any of the family dynamics I discussed earlier; for example one child I worked with was called sweetie pie by his mum, and this was used as a taunt against him to engage in the kicking of another player before he was 'exposed' or 'outed' to his friend who heard his 'pet name'.

What actually followed is the child's 'pet name' (shared in backdoor messages) was then used by his teammates after he carried this kicking action out, for which he felt betrayed, bullied and guilty for kicking his friend from the game. This resulted in a fight at school the following day after which the child was referred to my practice by school for aggressive behaviour and anger issues.

The underlying reasons were not, in fact, related to the playground fight but to a gaming issue that manifested in the real world. The story here is; this issue hadn't been seen (or asked about) by the teaching staff or parents, and they were primarily concerned about this child's anger issues. The child who had been 'kicked' had decided he would seek his revenge in person, and my client ended up talking to me about his feelings, which, of course, seemed justifiable for both parties in the fight and had been engineered by others. This had occurred on more than one occasion, and he was being set up in gaming events to create discord which spilled into the real world at school.

Stealing

Stealing items from another player's account is carried out for many reasons. Items that can be stolen are trophies, treasures or anything else that a player has accrued or created. These items or accolades can be taken for the prank, LOLs or simply because the opportunity is there to do so. To help you understand this, I will try to explain in simple terms; if you own a 'village' or 'world' such as those in Minecraft, you can allow people access to this space, through a link, which many children do to show their friends what they have achieved or built. This link-sharing is a bit like sharing a word document on Dropbox or Google Drive (if you're familiar with this). Have you ever told one of your friends in confidence where you are going out to an event, because you don't want others from the group to know, only to turn up to your event and there are the 'others' because your friend told them (by accident)? Did you feel frustrated and betrayed?

This is what it can be like for a child to be betrayed and have people enter their 'world' and then, to make matters worse for them, their items are stolen. This can also occur when the link is given to people unknown to the victim. They may not ever know who came and stole their items. They log back into their world, and their world has nothing left; it's been 'burgled'.

What would result in a child or young person conforming to a behaviour online through gaming? In this context, I'm going to use the phrase manipulator and manipulated. I'm then going to explain why in terms of attachment this is critical for understanding the process of the child. I'll use an example from therapy, although some of the details have been altered to prevent the identification of the child.

Scenario: A child is playing on an online game, and at some point an event within the house occurs that other players hear/see or find out about; this can be something like conversations in the background whilst the mic is on, the image that a camera captures, the gamertag that denotes age/sexuality/lifestyle choices, a piece of chat shared verbally or in writing or a reaction to something that happens in a game (e.g. crying/raging that is heard over the mic). At this point, no crime or issue exists, merely everyday gaming activities as seen and heard throughout the world.

A particular piece of information is then utilised by a manipulator and becomes one step in the process of exploitation. For example the manipulator here said that they saw a naked image of the child on the console camera or webcam. Now they wanted £10 or they'll show it to everyone. The manipulator may even use threats of 'You need to. . . [and insert a threat such as take another picture/video] or I will tell/show. . .' This is how money or sexual images become the currency that is traded as part of the exploitation. Often, with increasing fees or images/videos, often called sextortion, these sexual images are the currency.

Sometimes, the manipulators are told to 'go elsewhere' by fearless, tech-savvy or disinhibited young people. In therapy, there was a time when these words were uttered by an adolescent and sums this up fairly neatly:

> [I]t's like those people who sell the big issue, they approach you, you tell them piss off and they bother someone else, you just don't get the <u>have a nice day</u> bit.

For a child having the autonomy to say, 'Don't bother me', in terms of threats, harassment or manipulation is often difficult, especially when they are brought up with manners, social norms, told not so say no (because its rude/disrespectful/angers adults/shows them up and so on). Many are unable to speak about their feelings to others or adults or saying, "Hey I'm really uncomfortable with that, please don't . . ."

Fear often renders them unable to speak out. Fear is the biggest 'persuader' for a child to engage in behaviours. For example, the following quote is taken from the child client as we discussed her homelife and why her parents didn't know about this event:

> [T]his is why I will go to bed quietly, whilst my parents think I am obedient and inside I am terrified of making a sound as ***** (father's name) said he will beat me to death if I make another noise at bedtime and ruin his TV.

The child was terrified of many things at bedtime, and fear of being beaten to death was the highest on the list of issues, not the £10 manipulation. We managed this in therapy with the help of Dad, after he explained it was a joke and he didn't mean it. We talked about the impact the joke had on a brain that was less developed than his cognitive brain and had less of a sarcasm detection system.

My client was then able to talk about the threats to handing over money online, and we were able to find the manipulator who turned out to be someone on the other side of the world and was unlikely to carry out their threats as there had never been an image that they claimed to have. This is a common phishing technique used by cybercriminals (email scam), and of course, my client did not know this and was mortified to think this image existed and she could be blackmailed about it.

How do manipulators create this fear? It is a fairly simple process of tapping into the innate, natural and normal fear we all have of disconnection and rejection and being alone and feelings of shame. Fear taps into the attachment system. There is a great book that talks about the gift of fear by Gavin De Becker (2000), and in this book, he talks about the two major fears we have in terms of our biological sex.

However, these are fears that mature with social conditioning and are only applicable to adolescents and beyond. Younger children do not have these fears; they have primary human fear of I could die. Rejection also triggers this feeling and is underpinned by the need to be attached to another person to ensure their survival. So, if a person makes a threat to their life or someone else, this taps into the most innate function of the human brain and body: survive at all costs. When a child has an insecure attachment pattern this fear can be elicited very quickly and the threat response system that was covered in the first section of the book can find itself on high alert. This is where Amy R really shows up!

If the threat taps into the child's feeling of shame; for example an adult shouts with a face or voice (prosody) that reflects disappointment or rage, 'I can't believe you did that!!!' (usually denoting a shameful event) and 'Now I'm going to. . . (insert threat)', the compliance rate is going to be high. Point of note, it doesn't have to be a shameful event; you just have to make the recipient think it was shameful.

Shame is connected to how fear works in the brain and body, and it's how people are often recruited for purposes that can be in opposition to their belief system (e.g. radicalisation). Children (and adults) are susceptible to this fear and shame-based coercion, and if we educate them about this in terms of what people might do or say to try and persuade you, rather than here's how to avoid it (*many of the teachings around child abuse/grooming follow this particular pattern), we might just edge their critical thinking skills that bit more, develop that inner scientist and make it more likely that children and young people will want to turn to us and ask for advice.

Reflection

If you consider for a moment why I introduced the chapters on trauma, attachment and the polyvagal theory, I am hoping that you can see how primal survival behaviours are tangled into everyday online behaviours and how these can be manipulated, altered and exploited to create a hot soup of potential child abuses and genuine, normative mistakes made by children. You may be able to see how one small piece of information for their or your daily lives can be used to 'threaten' a child with coercive force/threat by potential criminals and perpetrators. These are often not professional criminals either but other children who are attempting to get their needs met in a way that harms your child. We don't see these behaviours as we would in the real world due to the amount of silent communication that occurs online through text, headphone chatting and the build-up to the events and so this a pause and think moment for us all, whether we are parents or professionals, It is time we took a deep interest in our child's online life.

What can we do as parents and professionals?

If you consider all the preceding, then what we do to help is reasonably easy to work out. We don't shame the child for making the decisions they did online or because they were feeling pressure to do so. They were scared, worried or more concerned with the avoidance of shame and, of course, being harmed by the manipulator's threats. Moreover, the team, clan or group you belong to can have a stress-inducing effect more strongly than outsiders of this group (Perry, 2009), and so children can feel more pressure if they know the manipulator. Many of us think we are brave and courageous. We like to think this about ourselves in this way because it affirms our power to be in control. However, so many pieces of research and findings highlight that in the face of fear, we are not always that brave and courageous person we thought we would be, and this is often what leads to the guilt, shame and embarrassment of trauma survivors. It can and is very disconcerting for some people to feel this, including these children, because it rocks your world and the supposition of who you thought you were.

Being empathic to the fear and shame is the solution and caring behaviour is what we need to exhibit to children here to create a connection with them and enable a conversation and corrections. Shame and fear are debilitating at times as they use the same part of the nervous system's responses and pathways as trauma (discussed in the stories earlier). We are not always the masters of our decisions and biology will always trump opinion, and so it should. We would die out as a species very quickly if we followed our slower thinking processes.

References

de Becker, G. (2000). *The gift of fear: Survival signals that protect Us from violence.* Bloomsbury Publishing LLC.

Knibbs, C. (2016). Banter and memes. *Respect Yourself.* https://respectyourself.org.uk/banter-memes-one-aspect-cybertrauma/

Perry, D. (2009). Examining child maltreatment through a neurodevelopmental lens: Clinical applications of the neurosequential model of therapeutics. *Journal of Loss and Trauma, 14*(4), 240–255. doi:10.1080/15325020903004350

11 It's not all bad

Examples from practice

Introduction

This particular chapter of the book has small vignettes from clients (with identities concealed) and people I have personally spoken with about the positives that gaming can bring. As discussed, this can be health, mental health, friendships, pain management, hospital visits, phobia issues, therapy and many of the benefits listed earlier.

To give you a brief look into the hows, they can be taking a walk to find items for the game such as Pokémon Go, the Wii Yoga or sports-type games and virtual reality games. People's mental health can improve by having people to talk to when you're lonely, isolated or incapacitated (bed-bound or housebound); it can improve through making companions online and supporting this social mechanism, which, in turn, helps us feel better. Remember, we are social mammals after all.

Playing games can help with distraction from pain and illness and can provide young people with a welcome distraction or learning about their visit when they attend hospital for invasive therapies or surgery. They can help with coordination after some surgeries. They can help with phobias or fears and allows a child to navigate an environment they may not physically be able to.

The reason I use computer-based games in therapy generally falls under two types, the health-based ones such as **biofeedback** and the play-orientated console games such as those I have been speaking about. The biofeedback ones are games that measure some form of biological response such as **heart rate variability** or **brain waves,** and these send a signal from the device the person wears (head/ear/wrist monitors) back to the computer or device for the client to pay attention to and change their biological or sensory behaviour accordingly (e.g. speeding up or slowing down of breath). It combines gamification of what would

DOI: 10.4324/9781003169390-13

otherwise be, more than likely, boring, distracting or, for those with anxiety, a provocative experience.

Console games come in a variety of styles and age ratings, and so I change, remove or adjust the settings and availability for the therapy interventions, which allows me to work with a particular issue. I talk, play alongside or against my clients. This helps me understand them and their issues more deeply, I get to learn about their worldview/approach and beliefs in a way that you cannot find out by talking alone. I can 'see' what they are doing, how they are doing it and, of course, how they navigate issues. For example, working with adolescents, I am able to see how they relate to themselves, what their self-beliefs are, how they socialise and how they believe their avatars should behave (when these are part of the game) or vice versa. With younger children for example I can see and work with emotional regulation issues, communication, self-limiting beliefs and family dynamics, depending on what game and console I am using. I find that this 'format' exceeds many of the interventions that I can use in play therapy alone and in isolation. As such, this mode of working has become my go-to and favourite way of working with my clients.

Now, if you were to believe the media then I would likely be telling you that every client who attends my practice with a 'gaming addiction' or 'disorder' who plays games in my room 'rages out' when we need to stop the game. I have never encountered this. Ever. I have encountered normative developmental issues such as time-wasting and delay tactics and all of the other behaviours that get exhibited when the children are having fun and don't want to leave, and this occurs with painting, using the sand tray, building Lego towers and any other activity we are engaged in during the session. I see these behaviours at the parks, zoos and playgrounds that children go to and have 'trouble leaving'. This is interesting to note the language here that is used, mostly by parents when they explain their child doesn't want to get out of the swimming pool or leave the park. As yet, I have not seen a child diagnosed with an outdoor-playing addiction. Do you ask yourself what is the world coming to when one behaviour in one domain is a mental health issue but it is not in another?

Examples from therapy: abuse, anxiety, divorce and injections!

Vignette: Laura was 13. She had recently been a victim of child sexual abuse by her peers, known as child sexual exploitation. She had recently attended the local National Health Service for some appointments but was discharged for her refusal to communicate with them. When she arrived at my therapy room, she asked me if I would behave like the previous therapist and ask lots of questions. I told her I would only be interested in her choices of what she would like to do in therapy, such as talk or play games, including computer games. She asked me which games I had, and we chose some very silly ones on the Nintendo Wii. These were ones she felt could actually 'do' (competence and success in therapy situations are very important in terms of agency and self-belief).

We decided to play Rayman Rabbid Series (very funny and silly games) and some of the sports-type games that needed two players. She was engaging in what we call cooperative play and we were turn-taking which is one the most basic needs of a conversation, connection and human behaviour. I shall not give away my therapy strategies here in a public book as they may be used out of context and by untrained people, but safe to say, the games had lots of joy, fun and failures, and this was a very coherent and therapeutic relationship facilitated by the games. As Laura worked through the games, we would dip in and out of her trauma in many ways, through words and non-verbal communication, and I was able to reflect back to her about the somatic issues I could see (biological, posture, breathing, prosody and safety behaviours), and I could monitor her eyes, face and proximity. I could match and regulate here and all the while having fun on the games with her. It was tremendous!

When you attend training to work with young people, it is often said to engage them in an activity that distracts them or one in which you are distracted such as driving so they will talk to you. As you are now aware that neuroception drives feelings of safety, so this can help explain the non-threatening eye contact in these situations. What I tend to do with gaming in therapy is pick a place to stand that communicates non-verbally that we are as safe as we can be (I pay attention to the cues that tell me where I need to be proximally), and I keep a particular distance that is (as best as can be) not threatening to a client's nervous system. I do not encroach within that personal space until it is safe to do so. You see, as a therapist using computer games, I respect their nervous system information as much as the actual gameplay.

Most children who play games at home, feel safer than they do in a therapy room when they sit across from a therapist. Therapy can be a strange situation to begin with, and as such, this is why specific training is paramount around this intervention as it is not 'just playing games'. Furthermore, there are **e-safety**, safeguarding and legal issues to contend with, but that's another book and in the courses that I teach.

Vignette: Jonny was 9 and was having a hard time at home as his parents were about to divorce. He was referred to me for 'angry outbursts at school'. His parents said he was quiet at home, never had any of the issues school reported and was a caring, considerate and a calm boy at home, apart from when they tried to get him to turn off Minecraft. Upon an assessment, it turned out that when we played Minecraft in therapy, Jonny could show me and talk me through his 'world' (metaphorical and the one he built in the game), where he felt he could be in control of what was happening, how he was the 'designer' of a world that was different to the real one he had no control over (the one in which his parents were divorcing). This real world often had lots of arguing, raised voices and distressing feelings accompanying it. Minecraft was Jonny's regulated and stable world; he felt psychologically safe here and did not have to think about things that were out of his control. He could play out different scenarios of what life might be like after the divorce.

In therapy, we continued the narrative that allowed him to work out what felt safe and how as his parents divorced what could be the parts of his life, he has control over (such as the clothes he took to or kept in each location). We decided to make an ideal world, a real world and a fantasy world and see what was similar, different and what he liked and could control throughout the worlds. This gave Jonny a feeling of power and emancipation, and autonomy in a world where children very rarely get these aspects.

Jonny's behaviour at school changed as he realised that school was very ordered and was unlikely to, in his words, 'let him down by rejecting and abandoning him, as his parents had'. This allowed Jonny to use the school as his safe base whilst the transitions occurred around him and until he could feel settled into a routine with his parents.

Why did he not want to leave his Minecraft world at home? It seems obvious now perhaps. He would have to face the reality of what was happening around him, which he was powerless and did not have the inner resources and tools to manage. Minecraft offered him refuge from these feelings. Jonny found these resources within himself throughout therapy, and this, in turn, allowed him to face the issue 'head on' knowing he had a way to understand and 'cope'. Minecraft became much easier to 'leave' as his real world was safer, more predictable and more reliable.

Vignette: Molly was 7. She came to my office with Mum and Dad and was presenting with panic attacks at school; she also had a skin condition that looked very similar to eczema. We looked at using the paints, computer games and the sand tray, but she decided that her hands might hurt in the sand or paint, so Molly decided to use games to explain what was going on for her. As we explored and navigated the challenges that faced her (in the games), we were able to look at her internal feelings of power. When we played **role-playing-games** (RPG), what did she have to use to overcome the problem, how did she use it, what happened to it once she had used it and how could she 'power up' once more?

We then looked at applying this to her anxiety symptoms and behaviours and how she could 'gamify' this into her real world. For example we looked at the 'baddies' she had to overcome in the game and how she was able to see her anxiety as one of these baddies that she could either put a spell on, silence, squash, and many more great ideas that she used from the games. Each idea came from a different game, and we tried to find as many ideas as we could so her magic bag was full of ways to beat the baddies.

Over a number of weeks, Molly was able to attend many of the situations she had previously avoided, been frightened of, such as going to the cinema, shopping and even attending a football match! Molly became the mage or as she called herself the "wizardess of wondefulness' (WOW!).

Vignette: Danny was 12, had Type 1 diabetes and was diagnosed as being on the autism spectrum disorder continuum (he was diagnosed with what used to be called Asperger's). He had to regularly attend hospital for tests and routine investigations. As he approached his 13th birthday, he began to suddenly fear the hospital and the injections. His parents became increasingly concerned about how they struggled to get him there as it was turning into a battle every time. Danny played a computer game I was familiar with from my younger years.

Years ago, the only way to play some of the games now computerised such as Warhammer and Bloodbowl was to use figures that you built, painted and then played on a tabletop (a little bit like Subbuteo). Danny was able to talk to me about the figures, clans and battles, and I could resonate with him around these. (I even brought one of mine in to show him.) I could be with him in his explanations of what he thought was happening at the hospital through conversations and asking questions of what it would be like for a character to do this in real life. We decided to design some new armour for his "Diabetic" Space Marine (which did cost his parents as they were in-app purchases, and we talked this through with them each time). We added the coolest weapons that helped him feel like he was the ultimate warrior and hero. As he was due to go to hospital for his next appointment, we worked out how he could take a version on his iPad, and for each injection or blood test, he could do something on his iPad to distract him whilst they took place. He had decided he would add something to his armour to show the success of his achievement and then show me in therapy the next session. By the end of our sessions, the Space Marine was one of the most highly decorated I have ever seen. Danny manages his appointments by playing with and, of course, 'upgrading' this Space Marine. Danny didn't stay long in therapy as it took little time for him to find a way to work with his issue.

Whilst some of the work here may have looked similar if for example I used the sand tray; I have no doubt that some of those interventions would not have been addressed as quickly as they were through gaming. There is something so spectacular and special about computer games and how children interact with them in play. They do so whilst knowing that this is a different form of make-believe with many real-world issues and concepts, making this a unique way of playing that is not understood fully by the world of adults – yet.

Gamers often 'get it' and struggle to see why non-gamers cannot. Hopefully now you do too. This is why we need to be wary of diagnoses and labelling of this particular form of play. It really is #gamingforgood and #play in a stunning form. Of course, there will be those times that cause problems, issues and heartache for families, and of course, I work with these issues in therapy and don't deny that there can be problematic ones at times. It is something we need to watch for, and the gaming disorder diagnosis has much to offer us in understanding why the World Health Organization considers it to be such a problem. However, as I was writing this book and we headed into lockdown, I wonder if it became a salvation and mental health space for young people to be with their mates and hold onto some of the social skills that they need for development and maturation.

In the last 2 years or so, another issue has become the prevalent conversation of academics, parents and the mainstream media, which is discussed in the next chapter.

12 Gambling in games

Is this the same as sticker books, competition or is it more sinister?

Introduction

I keep this chapter short due to time constraints and the fact that 'gambling', a legal issue in the UK, covered by the Gambling Act 2005, is to be updated in 2021, and of course, the book was written before then and so cannot cover what will emerge from the new act. To date, we are only just exploring this in terms of research and do not know the long-term impacts of this issue (much like all of them within the book). The issue with the law of gambling here is it was derived under the basis and applicable to activities for people who were 18 and legally old enough to use their own money on. It is, as I have said, an area that is currently being looked at by several organisations and academics.

However, this may take some time as there are so many variants of the 'things' that children can pay money or time for or take risks to win. When you consider that normative aspects of growing up are 'risk-taking', conflict and peer pressure, it muddies the water as to what is directly gambling behaviour (based on the same typologies as addiction) and what is developmentally appropriate or on the cusp of a pathology.

If you're old enough to have or work with children and are reading the book to help you understand young people, then you may remember the Panini sticker books, Pokémon cards, Adidas, Nike or Reebok sportswear, snapbacks, Beyblades, Tamagotchis, scented erasers and/or schoolwork results (tests/exams or homework). What do these have to do with gambling? They have all likely, at some point, for some children involved dares, cheats or risk-taking in order to 'win' one of them. We create a world of having it all by setting our children up with competition which includes winning, losing and taking risks. Michael Jordan, David Beckham and Connor McGregor have created careers out of taking risks and 'betting on the odds'.

DOI: 10.4324/9781003169390-14

When this becomes a problem and, of course, this can be a large financial one for some families is when the risk-taking and betting on the odds results in a failure to stop when the negative effects are taking a toll on the family (maybe financially) and perhaps at the detriment to a child's mental, physical and emotional well-being. Under these circumstances, Gabor Mates's reflection is suitable here, more so than some of the other issues with and around gaming. Although I add in my cautionary point from the earlier as to the underlying patterns and motivations, gambling is often more of a negative outcome and effect due to it being linked to in-app purchases and monetary buying of unknown packages, which, of course, can be seen to be a burden in the real world on a bank, phone or credit card statement.

I would like to reiterate something that I discussed earlier about the cognitive and regulatory abilities of children under the approximate age of 12 and remind the reader that the ability to critically think, analyse and plan for consequences is difficult to assess and, of course, connect to behaviour as a planned intention in this age group. When we look to gambling diagnoses, they resemble addiction in the need to have this intention present. We are currently in a space in time when we are collecting research based on outcomes rather the phenomenology (a person's experience and meaning) of 'why'.

Like 'hook-a duck', the prizes (**lootboxes**, packages, skins) can be on show, whereas the subtler forms of taking risks may include time spent on the game or taking a risk with your experience (XP) points. As these are not always monetary children are sometimes swayed by others or the lure of a better item versus the 'risk' of losing something. Peer pressure can be a real part of this such as the example of the child who 'bought' a cheat code from a peer who told them it would unlock 'packs'. It turned out to be a code that locked him out of his Xbox account. Permanently. Did he gamble? Yes, he took a risk. Did he gamble in the same way as a poker or pontoon player? Yes. With the same cognitive intent? And is it a pathology? I will leave you to decide.

What I can talk about here is risk-taking and how children and adolescents think about the world in different ways. So let's go back to attachment styles: children with a secure attachment style are regulated in both nervous system and thinking styles. They will and are able to take managed risks and often weigh up the outcome. This does not mean that they will not take risks that are based on chance outcomes, however. The idea of winning something is quite innate in all of us, and of course, many adults buy lottery tickets with this 'hope'. Secure attachment allows the child to accept losses and (hopefully) move on without feeling the need to 'keep playing' with a feeling of hope. They are likely to be able to ask parents or carers for the item they wish to attain, buy or gamble for within a game. They are likely to be able to handle disappointment and loss and can recover from this fairly quickly with little or no lasting effects −on most occasions.

Children who have an insecure attachment style do not think, behave and believe in this way. They are more likely to engage in behaviours without checking about their consequences and are unlikely to be able to see the future impacts of their choices (as this requires a style of thinking that is the opposite of regulation, patience and deliberation). There is less inhibition to risky behaviour and more compulsion to feel like a wanted, needed person or a 'winner'.

This means that the children with this attachment style are going to see the outcome as being one that will advance their status, XP points or credibility with their friends. This feels like a choice about wanting to be in a relationship and is exactly what this attachment style is about. In turn, this is likely to create and drive a yearning and desire to have the item (skin, etc.) so that they can be wanted, needed or seen by the 'in-group' and liked by their friends. It's a drive to build a bigger, stronger and reliable survival network and not so much about 'having everything' (although this is a real feeling too). It is based on risks related to winning so that there are more people to connect with. It's about belonging. Underneath it all, it is about attachment. If you ask a child with this attachment style, why they do almost anything but take risks, there is always a story that encompasses others that they are trying to connect, play and be with.

When is it risk-taking, hyper-rational thinking or gambling?

What is **hyper-rational thinking**? This was first brought to my attention by Dr Dan Siegel (2014) and is a description of a thinking style that is more prevalent in adolescents. It is a way to think about the odds, where they 'look' in the favour of a win. It is a cognitive comparison to the odds of 'not winning'. When this is the case, that's when they will likely take a chance or risk. For example running an amber light is something many adult drivers have done; however, they are less likely to run a red light because they implicitly understand the chances of cars coming in the other direction who will be on green. The outcome in this circumstance is in the odds of 'crashing and being badly hurt'.

However, an adolescent will consider the chances and comparison of 'I gambled with this before; it didn't happen to me then, so there's a good chance and good odds it won't this time either'. We hear this as 'it won't happen to me', and often, in education, we spend our time showing children the worst that could happen, only for it to fall on hyper-rational ears. I wonder if you just considered (rationalised) why this thinking is flawed. I wonder if you know this is likely due to a few factors of your own maturation: you saw someone crash or get hurt in this way, or you now realise your thinking, planning and reasoning has to include your family and other people around you. One of the differences between us and children and young people is we have responsibilities which can become our inner chatter and change the way we think about our decisions and behaviour. Young people often do not see they have responsibilities.

Hyper-rational thinking, also known as risky behaviour decisions, is why many children steal a biscuit or £1 out of the purse/wallet because they didn't get caught last time, so as far as they are concerned 'the odds are in their favour' and 'you're less likely to notice one, or perhaps two. Maybe three, but that's pushing it, no? And surely you won't be that angry, will you? Not for one biscuit?' And, of course, younger children do not have the capacity to think in the same way and often think they won't get caught, period.

So, children will take risks (also known as gambling) and the designers of games would do well to consider that packs, packages, skins and so on will be used, bought and chased after. Perhaps even more so than in the adult game market. Monetary gain has often been a moral sidestep in a consumerist world and the children often pay the price for this when it is considered above their well-being. We can do better.

Reference

Siegel, D. (2014). *Brainstorm. The power and purpose of the teenage brain.* Jeremy P Tarcher.

Social media: relationships in the palm of your hand

The what, why and how to help

13 Does technology, social media or our devices have an impact on mental health?

Introduction

There's a joke about bears and where they go to the toilet, so I'll just state the obvious here. Yes, technology has an effect both positively and negatively. Does it cause as is suggested in the media and by some academics, unhappiness, depression or anxiety? In one word, no. In fact, we don't actually know what *causes* any of these issues, and to be perfectly honest, we take very well-educated guesses at leading or contributory factors to many issues, but no one actually knows what causes anything (other than in sciences like physics or chemistry and even that's up for debate). This is where research is helpful because we can find things, factors or variables that contribute, are correlated or associated with, and rarely do we find *the cause* when it comes to human bodies, minds or behaviours.

How can we say that digital devices or technology are the cause or to blame when adults have been using computers for the last 20-plus years for work purposes? An environment such as the workplace, a boss or perhaps pressures to perform, such as sales per quarter, are often said to be the cause of work-related stress, not the devices that workers use. The same kind of thinking often surrounds young people in education when we say it's exam stress and not the fact they have to stare at computers, screens or interactive whiteboards all day. Could it be there are multiple factors at play here? It seems paradoxical to me that we blame technology when we use it to support us in work, yet I have not seen to date, this 'issue' in the media as a leading cause of mental health distress. The following pathology highlights this:

> Using your computer, screen or device to process your spreadsheet data for this week's sales will cause mental health issues, depression anxiety and rage. Spreadsheet addiction and disorder can be seen in workers who are found to spend over 35 hours per week interacting

DOI: 10.4324/9781003169390-16

with Excel and inputting numbers and find themselves unable to not use it daily whilst at work. Features of this disorder include tutting, finger-tapping, leaning towards the screen, excessive mouse scrolling and keyboard tapping. Users can become enraged if interrupted or asked to answer the phone during a vital stage of input. Research in this area finds users unhappiness rating increased towards the end of the tax year and this has led researchers to believe that cumulative, excessive and daily use of Excel is the leading contributor to this disorder. Line managers would do well to approach users carefully in the workplace in case of outbursts which include items from the desk being launched in their general direction. To overcome this disorder, users must be admitted to an Excel detox facility provided by Catherine Knibbs at £150,000 per week.

I shall be sensible now and return readers to the line about technology and digital devices being a medium and a tool. I wholeheartedly acknowledge that problematic use of anything can be a real issue. I wouldn't be in the job I am if I thought otherwise. As discussed earlier it is often our use of a tool or intentions behind using a tool that 'maketh the issue'. For example, toasters are a tool. If you toast bread with them by placing square and aptly sized slices of bread into it, you will be provided with toast. However, if you stick a knife into the heating elements or put soup in it you can guarantee, it won't provide you with toast, and the outcome will be vastly different to the first scenario. And so, the metaphor behind the use of tools (or toasters) lends itself to mental health in terms of devices, technology and apps.

Use, misuse of tools: do you read the instruction manuals?

There's no instruction manual for many forms of technology, not the kind about what to do 'in/through them' anyway, and this is where this book comes in. We have as a species (mostly) blindly started using technology without knowing what could have, would have, might have and is now happening. What does this hold for us in the future too?

What is a concern, in terms of what I see on referral forms and what I see my clients for, are the issues that arise as a result of using this tool or the impact from the relationship issues created, crafted and broken with, in and through this tool. Often, these are not so different from corporeal world issues. For example, I work with clients who have gambling issues from casinos as well as online poker, and this has an impact on relationships in their life regardless of the 'location' of the gambling. I work with children who have been bullied in school, online or both, and this influences their self-esteem.

So, when I am asked about the impact technology has on a person's mental health, I ask the question, What is the significant factor that makes this a technology-only issue? Because virtual, electronic or digital-based life is much the same as the corporeal world, it is difficult to separate these as has been discussed in the book so far. Language also confuses the landscape here when attempting to work with issues that come into my therapy room as the world of technology has been in the words, behaviour and lives of my clients for many years now. I see no distinction between what people do with, on, around and in technology because every session includes a conversation about every aspect of a client's world – even those in their 70s! TV, radio and technology are as much a part of a session as feelings, diet and hobbies can be. Is it time we stop making a distinction of technology being a thing to demonise and see human beings behaving in a world that is facilitated (not always positive) but supported by and through technological advances?

For example, I often see the words **'digital native'** (Prensky, 2001) used to refer to someone who has been born into the digital age or after the invention of the iPhone or, conversely, the **digital immigrant** who was born before this time. I understand why this term (*native*) was introduced; however, we have not really applied this use of language to other tools such as kettles, irons, showers, gym equipment, cars and so on, have we? I haven't been aware of a child who is a toaster native or myself a toaster immigrant or a gym native or gym immigrant. I am aware though that when we first begin to describe and name potential issues in and around research, we find a name that seems appropriate and applicable. So we have these terms for now (along with *silver surfer* and a few more). To be honest I class myself as a technological native because my use has extended to almost all my life, beginning with my Fisher Price Telephone and cot activity set. Learning to use the TV probably came shortly after, and since then I have lived 'here' and joined the internet space when all the other adults did too, who, by the way, invented this technological life that the natives were born into.

When you think about a native, you think about someone who is a local and has many of the habits that their environment creates, for example, an accent or colloquialism, or an outfit for the surroundings, for example warm clothing for cold climates. This is usually an evolutionary adaptation to their surroundings and can take place very quickly. This is exactly what I have been seeing in users of the virtual world; they are creating their own language such as 'googling', which by now most of us know is to search for something on the internet regardless of the search engine or site we use. We have adapted our opposable thumb ability to type whilst holding a device in our hands. You might want to take a moment to just watch a young person's motor skills doing this; it's amazing. I'm not so sure about the outfits to be honest, but if the TV programme *Big Bang Theory* is anything to go by, then perhaps it's T-shirts? Maybe the technology users are indeed easy to spot using this approach. Or perhaps they are seen 'in the wild' carrying a little device that they look at, put to their head and tap a lot? Maybe then, for at least 50 years or so, we will still be using the *native* and *immigrant* terms to determine those who are born before the internet revolution in the 1990s and after it.

Mental health and technology

What I consider to be a more pertinent question in today's world is how life through technology affect, change or support mental health and well-being rather than the apportion of blame onto technology itself or the platforms used. When you consider what has been discussed so far, you can see that this is an overlapping of spaces inhabited by young people (and adults) like a Venn diagram. It is how they 'live' there that parallels how they live in this real, corporeal world. We currently only have a small minority of technology-related studies to draw on compared to, let's say, research into social groups, cognitive thinking and the psychodynamic world of attachment. Yet, in the media, we are seeing so many frightening, doom-based and negative stories. Much of this research comes from self-reported measures directly and indirectly from users with little consistency and replication. Much of the research that exists at this present time is like a pilot study in which we have only had the internet for a fraction of our lives in terms of a bigger picture of human development.

In neuroscience, we talk about the decade of the brain, and in this time, we have learned quite a lot about the differentiation, localisation and interactions of certain areas, but in truth, we know very little. The brain, if you remember, has so many connections that it is going to take us a very long time to understand this fully, if at all ever. If we apply the same thinking to the human population, which currently stands at approximately 8 billion, we have a very large number of human behaviours in the real world, let alone the changing pace and landscape of what technology offers us in terms of communication, connection and interactions.

Technology itself has already changed the way we communicate as a species, in terms of information collection, distribution and speed and disinformation, misinformation and varying versions of the truth.

Political and environmental changes across the world have taken place alongside technology and this has impacted accessibility, availability and social inclusion. What was once perhaps conceived as a (simple) system for browsing information has become a new world of human behaviour. In today's climate, this has produced a space for harmony, polarisation, shared experiences, differences and a new evolution of connection and what this means for the human that is evolving in a world where this virtual space intrudes, overlaps and changes the brain.

The ability of our brains to change and adapt to new and novel stimuli is called neuroplasticity, or being 'soft-wired' (Merzenich, 2013), and we are in the infancy of this synchronised and synthesised process with technology and the virtual space, with yet-to-be-discovered mechanisms for studying this robustly. I'm going to suggest that there is indeed an evolving connectivity between cyber synapses and people facing the screen, facilitated by the virtual or digital space. It's not necessarily all negative, and the long-term impact is one that we cannot accurately predict. We cannot say where technology is currently taking us given the sudden explosion of the iPod to smartphone speeds, **augmented** and **virtual** reality and **haptic feedback** systems (bodily sensations via clothing/suits etc.) appearing on the horizon. What we must do is keep researching the current impact on health and well-being for us to understand how technology changes us.

Technology isn't going to fix an inherently human problem. How we are, how we live and how we connect seem to be the most important factors for change and helping our children, not more technology; that will fight fire with fire. However, there is certainly a place for technology to assist with issues, and that's a different conversation to be had.

What do we mean by mental health?

When we consider mental health (MH), we are also looking to a phenomenon that can mean several things, and we haven't quite managed to define this yet in a world without technology. Do we mean the absence of an MH disorder, do we mean we to feel healthy, or do we mean that our brains are absent of physical issues? Language once again becomes so important in this aspect. In 2017, there was an article that appeared in the mainstream that almost 'blamed' the iPhone for young people's levels of unhappiness and depression. In consideration of the researcher's intention, I think perhaps the goal was to show that the introduction of the smartphone had resulted in young people feeling less satisfied with their lives and more pressure from the impact of this technology because of what was communicated through this space. Whilst unhappiness and depression are two very different sides of the same coin, they are also not the full picture on MH as a definition either. What was missing from this research was, and is to date, the meaning and aspect of a child's life with the inclusion of technology rather than using this as the variable by which to measure.

I think the space of social media has allowed research like this to take the headlines, (negativity bias in action!) and has resulted in public arguments by other researchers, and this can confuse the public. In turn, this results in both moral and pragmatic panic without due cause. I have personally encountered in practice some professionals with worries and anxieties about children's use of technology with phrases such as 'but it's been proven, Cath' or 'I read on. . .' (the only thing you can actually 'prove' by the way is bread).

So what does this mean for parenting?

What does this mean for us as parents and professionals? How do we manage this information and apply it to our parenting, education and safeguarding of children and young people? How do we manage risks, dangers, the idea of recommended screen time (which we now know is poot) and what is the impact or damage that occurs? How do we manage this in our families, school and places they go and provide a good basis for helping our children grow with this technology? How can we protect our children and young people from any harmful or negative effects or consequences?

In truth, all we can do is use the tools we have at the time and use these to the best of our ability. We are not superhuman, and there are currently lots of people working hard to produce apps and interventions to help us do this. However, we as parents and adults must learn about the technology, terminology and current research to help us make informed decisions rather than media-driven panics. Easier said than done, right? Where are the resources among the noise, and what do we do if these 'events' or 'effects' happen? I am aware we as parents and professionals have limited time to spend researching, and we need it made simple, delivered quickly and with a robust underpinning. We are busy people!

References

Merzenich, M. (2013). *Soft-wired. How the new science of brain plasticity can change your life.* Parnassus Publishing.

Prensky, M. (2001). Digital natives, digital immigrants part 1. *On the Horizon, 9*(5), 1–6. https://doi.org/10.1108/10748120110424816

14 Social media and dis-order

Introduction

What about the manipulation, the dis-order of information produced, consumed and shared? Let's talk about critical thinking, as a skill and a time-consuming method of belief.

Since the dawn of man, we are said to be teachers and students, parents and children. We have passed on our skills of survival, knowledge, humour and negativity bias to the next generation through a skill set of disciplines, storytelling, pictures, images and curiosity of our own life experiences. You only need look at any evolution or history books to see what I mean. If you read neuroscience-orientated books, you can see a discussion of how our brains evolved to have certain traits that helped us survive; this is often called the negativity bias. In short, this means that we are always more alert to the negative things around us, as Rick Hanson (2013, 2020) calls it the 'Velcro for taking in the bad and the Teflon for good'.

If we see, feel or hear something that could be bad for us, oh boy, do we make sure we pay attention to it (our life could depend on it), and herein lies the issue when it comes to the transmission of knowledge and the experiences through social media, internet forums, mainstream media and information shared by and through psychological games. If you spend much time in this 'online village', you're likely to see and hear more information than would be expected from a (non-technological) village, such as those who are still hunter-gatherer societies, or those who live in poverty-stricken areas and countries. Accessibility and availability create much more noise in the system that you would need to pay attention to.

For example, if you had to listen to the daily news by superfast fibre optic speeds of delivery versus a cassette tape that needs rewinding first, which one do you think you would prefer to use, would pay attention

DOI: 10.4324/9781003169390-17

to and would take the most information from? And so, short, fast-paced bursts of negativity bias and likely adrenaline spiking headlines will win the attentional economy, negativity bias and that orienting response I talked about earlier. This ensures Amy R is collecting the 'what-ifs' for us in the background and creating a doomsday list which she can refer to in a flash which is often called an amygdala hijack (Goleman, 1996), now sometimes called a limbic hijack.

Type I and Type II errors: statistics made easy

How our minds work and these shortcut processes they take keep us alive and functioning in today's busy world. However, minds can often make two types of mistakes known as **type I and II errors** (also reflected in the language of research): believe the truth when it's false and believe the falsity when it's true. There is a great book on this subject of thinking processes, errors and biases called *Thinking Fast and Slow* by Daniel Kahneman (2012), which is a more detailed version of the following explanation, which I am simplifying for you here:

> We humans don't like to take our time and figure out if there is an error of chance on what we see, read, or feel. Unless we stop, assess and carefully weigh up the evidence, which takes time (which we may not have), we often just believe what we are told, feel, think without checking the facts. This is what gossip, fake news, fantasies and rumours can look like. We live around this sort of content all our lives, so this is nothing new just because of the advent of social media. However social media exacerbates this flurry of misinformation, disinformation and misunderstood information. Sorting the wheat from the chaff takes effort or established expertise in a subject matter.

From infancy to the grave, we are fed inconsistent, fake and altered facts such as the games of 'got your nose' and peekaboo, Father Christmas and the Tooth Fairy. We learn facts at school that we cannot challenge; we are fed stories of our culture, society and religions; and until we have the capacity to investigate this for ourselves, we can only assume the 'tutors' and storytellers to be true. If we question the truth, we are given more facts or fantasy to challenge our cognition resulting in us feeling like we are wrong or incorrect. Therefore, what we have just been told 'must' be the truth because our parents, family, friends, teachers and politicians wouldn't lie to us, would they?

This is not about critiquing parents who tell stories of Santa but an analysis of the process of how children's thinking develops. For children younger than 7, there is magical and fantasy thinking (imagination), and reality is often queried with the question we all know and love from our small people: 'Why?' This is a normative stage of child development according to theorists such as Jean Piaget (1896–1980) and Donald Winnicott (1896–1971), who wrote about this separately over their careers. For some of us, we are excited by this question because our curiosity is nurtured, and for others, we stop asking why due to trauma, family dysfunction or being consistently shut down. It is only when adults help children challenge how the world works, educates and informs them that a child can begin to gain a deep understanding of the complexities of the systems in which they live.

Groupthink and going with the flow

Much of the time in our families, villages, schools, workplaces and society we go along with the majority to ensure we are not rejected or ejected from the tribe. It feels safer to believe the most common themes first and have the facts proved wrong later. Would you rather be incorrect and survive in your tribe, apologising later if facts turn out to be incorrect, or would you rather take your time, debate, reason, analyse and risk looking a 'clever clogs and know it all' and be rejected, discounted or disowned from the group? A study carried out in the 1950s showed a high percentage of people conformed to observable, direct lies to feel part of the group and not the outcast. (Asch, 1951 cited in Hogg & Vaughn, 2005). To be human is to sometimes to deny absolute facts in order to survive in your group.

What do you think most people do when they see something in the media, news or on social media? Do you check your facts when an article favours a view you hold? What about if the article angers you in some way, for example an injustice has been carried out or when a child or animal is hurt, injured or killed? What about a scary story such as 'all parents need to be aware of this new trend, game, person' or 'violent games cause violence in children'?

Do you take that information at face value and consider it to be true before checking the facts? Do you check the facts? Do you need to check the facts? And, when emotionally charged, do you share posts, videos, images, articles or gossip without checking the facts before doing so?

What is critical thinking, and why do we (mostly) not do it?

Critical thinking is an ability to weight evidence, debate, reason, challenge and assimilate an answer with the information to hand. It can mean thinking 'out of the box', using what is called logical and lateral thinking processes and being able to see many sides of the information presented. It creates a harmony between opposing thoughts and rationalises to come to an answer. This takes time and effort. It is generally not taught in education, or until a child has the cognitive abilities to do so, at approximately 12 years of age (Siegel, 2014), and of course, the discussion on adolescence and brain wave states will be a marked stage of this process too. What lessons do we provide for our children in the home and education that help develop creative and critical thinking? Is it true that it's only in science, technology, engineering and maths that scientific thinking is encouraged? How do we encourage this in all children in all aspects of life? Why would we, and for what purpose? Wouldn't this create a world of having to answer questions all the time?

It seems that parenting is full of this time-consuming question answering, and sometimes parents need to get on with work or life and do not have time for all of this. As said earlier, it is easier to fact-check later, and of course, stories handed down by families often go unchecked so as not to 'upset the apple cart'. We like to be efficient, get on with stuff and are not bad parents for doing this.

Knowing what your children consume online can also take time, and I have been told in therapy that parents don't have time to do this every day; they are busy people working and looking after their families. They often do not discuss with their children what they are reading, watching or talking about. This can be due to a few factors, and the one I hear most is 'it's boring as little Sammy goes on about Minecraft or Fortnight for the 50th time today'. Often, parents and children are not having conversations about the information they consume, children are told to be quiet when they bring up the digital space 'events of the day' or some parents do not understand the digital spaces, cannot hear or see what is being said to their child (e.g. headphones on) or have never looked at their daily interactions to sift through what could be facts, disinformation and misinformation. Your own relationship to technology and the enthusiasm you do or do not have for it can also affect how you talk to your child about their interactions with the content there.

Does your style of parenting affect your child's experience online?

Knowing how you parent can be helpful in terms of your own relationship with technology and how you see this in your family dynamics. Have you ever asked yourself what kind of parent you are? For example, are you authoritarian or liberal? Do you fear technology or embrace it? Do you penalise your children with technology? For example, when I was younger, the go-to and most used form of punishment for children seemed to be 'No TV or being grounded'. I can remember that it felt miserable, although I'm not sure it changed my behaviour and I got exceedingly good at saying sorry in order to reduce my 'time for the crime'. Nowadays, I see Wi-Fi codes changed, console bans and smartphone confiscations (schools also engage in these techniques). In my 2016 guidebook, I talked about some of the children who experienced this and their feelings.

'Digital parenting': the new paradigm?

Being human and being a parent can be difficult at times, and this book is not meant to highlight failings; rather, it is a research-driven approach for you and the child or young person you may be interacting with and can now apply this learning to or with. This book is written for all of us so we can understand what is a happening in terms of digital, electronic and virtual spaces and environments, whether we are a parent, carer, professional or indeed family relative we can help our children and ourselves navigate this changing world.

We certainly have permission to have not made the best parenting decisions so far, permission to get things wrong in the future and permission to increase our tools of connection and compassion in order that as we move forward in life surrounded and dominated by technology, that we are able to choose from our toolbox of knowledge. I often let my clients in therapy know that our ability to do our best is only based on the tools we have at the time. If we can increase our toolbox to have an assortment of choices or interventions and so on, then we can decide how we would like to act the next time.

Parenting in today's world means we need to update our skills and knowledge because previously we never needed to consider a cyber or technological-based world, and we know very little at this stage about the long-term impacts of where we are or heading. It hasn't been 'long term' yet as 25 years is a drop in the ocean of human behaviour research. We know something about where we will progress to in the next 10 years and based on Moore's law (2006), which is the speculation that computing power will increase exponentially (this is a simplistic reflection of his law); there's no real way we can accurately predict where we will end up, so we are left to only guess. No one knows what the next breakthrough or idea is until it happens.

What kind of parent are you, and what issues do you need to know about?

The research and science point towards attachment as the foundational Rosetta stone of body and brain development, interpersonal relationship harmony and connection between child and parent. This is how I help the families in therapy maintain a balanced and healthy style of parenting now that the digital age is here.

There are several parenting styles, and these can be applied to being around technology and can help us see how and why we approach an issue and what we think is best for our children. These approaches can also be influenced by culture, religions and, of course, other people around us (in real life and on our own technology). There is no right way to parent; however, there is always room for improvement. (Just ask the children.)

I'm going to throw a few phrases out here that are currently in use in memes or in the media. They are from teachers, tutors, coaches, professionals and parents, and I hope that you can bear with me whilst I present a slight satirical aspect to these phrases to illustrate how language shapes our approach to technology and the problems that arise.

These are as follow:

Digital Parenting: as in looking after, guiding and feeding a 1 or 0 till it reaches the age of 256 or 1 TB.

Digital Detox: as in electrons or Electro Magnetic Frequencies (EMF) or 1s and 0s being removed and excreted from our bodies or brains. Consumption of 1s and 0s? What is the poison here?

Digital Overload: as in phones are too heavy and result in #textneck or #ihunch. What is this equated to? Why do companies design smaller and smaller, then revert to larger phone sizes, and is it because of this?

Digital Dementia: as in you can't remember where your phone is, a term which I find disrespectful to those who have this brain-altering disease (that results in the loss of the humanness of a person, their memories and families along with it), but hey, the mainstream media and writers of books who named this are perhaps going for maximum impact.

Digital Distraction: as in the sentence I was going to type, but then I . . .

Digital Reputation: as in where/how you rate your devices; I mean, just how good are they?

Digital Tattoo: as in a microchip-shaped or like a bionic-looking one; an ink-based image on your arm or chest showing your love for consoles, gadgets, programs or organisations; or something as sinister as the marks left by concentration camps. (Yes, this did completely change the tone of this typology.)

Digital Identity: as in 1,0,0,1,1,0,1,0,1,1,1,0,1 or ASCII or the unique number the tax office or government has that tells them who you are.

And of course, the evolution of language itself: what happened to the previous terminology beginning with tech, electronic, online, cyber or internet-related and why is everything suddenly "digital" or "I" (as in iOS)? Will we soon move to saying virtual, immersive or augmented before discussing online spaces? Does this mean that we will be using new language, and will it change based on the media and research conducted at that time or perhaps based on a new course or intervention designed by an expert willing to treat the issue? I can find several courses very quickly online regarding the list earlier, and I wonder what it is the experts 'do' to 'rid you of these problems'?

It can be difficult to see the person in the issue when we use words like *digital*. When we look at children and young people, it can be easy to see the device as the villain of the story and forget that any behaviour the child or young person engages in seems natural to them or is a product of conditioning and culture or, as discussed, the manipulation by large tech companies to create this behaviour. In one aspect, the tech companies do create much of this behaviour in us because they have taken psychology, sociology and anthropology and used these theories to create a space and life that we buy into because we are human and not digital. We have feelings that can be toyed with, evoked and provoked, and the tech companies are doing the best they can to utilise the technology with the experts to create what they need; customers.

Privacy by default? What information is collected about customers (children)?

Speaking to children in therapy has often left me surprised at the number of devices, apps and platforms they use, download or try without parental knowledge about what they are or what they do with the information in the background. When it comes to online behaviour two elements that need considering regarding children are privacy and consent. The easy way to describe this is as follows: this about your child's right not to have their navigation online 'followed' by organisations or have information collected by companies about them without their or your permission.

When children engage in online activities, they will be using something designed by someone else in an organisation, for example Microsoft Word, Google search, PlayStation network, Apple App Store. Consent is also wrapped up in the dynamics of privacy and what this means, which is not always understood by children or young people. This becomes more complicated when they have no real concept of why privacy issues and consenting (agreeing) to something may have an impact on them. For example, a 7-year-old cannot understand what it will be like to be 12 and so cannot say they understand their rights as to why a company needs to process their data or collect this for their future activities. It's unlikely adults can imagine who they will be in a decade, so how can a young person project temporally and consider the decision about their data when they cannot 'do' this until they can cognitively and critically think? We as adults need to consider who may be taking their data (information about them), considering what for and how it can be used for or against your child. Why does a company need these data, and are they essential to the provision of the service?

Giving out information online: private or privacy?

Many children are taught mixed messages when they are young in terms of don't speak to a stranger, but if you're lost, go and speak to an adult such as a police officer, store assistant or woman (a stranger), followed by 'don't give out your address to anyone but give it to an adult if perhaps you are lost'. We also model this when we get into taxis with children and give our address to a stranger driving the car.

I'm aware I'm taking a cynical and extreme end of these views here, but often, children can become confused by advice such as keep your information private but give the platform the information it demands. Consent and privacy are the two areas that are mostly mixed up by well-intentioned adults hoping to help children be good 'digital citizens'. So how do we teach or explain these concepts?

Consent is often associated with sexual activity or as is the case since 2018, a requirement (on most occasions) in a European data protection law called the General Data Protection Ruling. It means to give permission for someone to 'process' your data (do something with them like add it to a database or mailing list). In research, we tend to ask for informed consent, which means to fully understand what you are committing yourself to and agreeing willingly to the process in the research. How is a child supposed to know the subtleties of what they are being asked for online if it is jargon or misleading? What about if it's an in-app purchase in a game or platform? How do we as parents explain the world online as being one which collects information about them and can potentially misuse it for targeted adverts, media feeds and, of course, creating the perfect space for a future customer?

Or is it the parents' and carers' responsibility to monitor this, as most of them pay the bill for the device or any other costs of online purchasing?

I have been teaching therapists and youth workers for the last few years about data protection, privacy, consent and security measures to prevent this from being stolen by cybercriminals, and I have a hard enough time communicating this in a way that creates clear and concise explanations that they understand. I have no doubt that most parents in today's world are not asking the questions I do of companies, apps, platforms and people in technology. If this is not communicated to my profession and beyond clearly, how can a parent or teacher explain it to a child?

I decided to squeeze this section in here for two reasons: first, because I teach this and my presence around children's data collection, privacy and consent became quite prevalent particularly since the lockdown of 2020. With many practitioners struggling with this or not knowing enough, I felt it imperative that it was included here.

Second, during the lockdowns, four tech giants – Apple, Amazon, Facebook and Google – were called to the US Congress to answer questions about issues relating to data. By now you will more than likely have heard of the Cambridge Analytica scandal and the interviews with Mark Zuckerberg that followed. In terms of my critical thinking approach, I found the actual interviews rather funny as the questions that were asked of Mark Zuckerberg et al. clearly showed people who didn't understand cyberspace and technology asking them to explain elements that they then further didn't understand. This is often why children call anyone over the age of 30 a boomer (most of us just don't get it!).

To give you an understanding of this issue as it relates to children and consent/privacy, there are now organisations such as 5Rights that are making systemic changes to the digital world to ensure that children's rights are protected by default online. Their tireless work has been shaping the world to come for those who will enter this space in the years to come and perhaps this will reduce some of the issues contained in this book (I hope). There's far too much to squeeze in this book; otherwise, this would become a whole book dedicated to the rights of children online and the challenges we face today, and of course, this book is introducing you to some of these issues here.

What are the risks, dangers and realities then?

The internet was never really designed with children in mind, nor did we design a child-friendly version, and even if we had, how would we monitor and police it, ensure that it was only ever frequented by children and that adults didn't enter their internet and children never entered the adult's worlds? The risks and dangers mirror those found in the real world. There are spaces that adults go to and behave like adults and our children can now get into these spaces by various means such as lying about their age or metaphorically sneaking in. These ideas are discussed within the next two chapters.

I am often heard to say that we gave children an unknowing all-access pass to an 18-plus world, rather like a nightclub, cinema, casino or adult sexual 'club' without knowing about or considering the consequences. We did not slow down and think and created something that many of us as adults were excited about, wanted to play with and use and, of course, which, developed by adults, was a space that wasn't considering the children who might appear there sooner than expected. Had we considered the internet as a new village, we could have used anthropological and historical knowledge of human behaviour and potentially designed '*safety lanes*' and '*stop*' buttons (not real things but a metaphor). We let the ever-increasingly intelligent beast loose, and we are now attempting to tame it by creating more technology to fight it with.

We are struggling to evidence the long-term impact and the world of cyberspace moves much faster than research. Therefore, we are ultimately always playing catch up. There's still a big divide in terms of speculation about the benefits and or damage of this technology. Currently, I sit with a view of there are indeed harms, risks and dangers, and many of these already exist in the real world where perpetrators of crimes exist, and we already have the research, and so the digital landscape should be similar in terms of humans frequenting these spaces.

For a moment, I will embrace my role as a therapist to say that we cannot and do not know the full impact (positive or negative) on the developing human in the technological, internet or digital age yet. Perhaps we could embrace the understanding that throughout history errors of judgement are made and that the speculation, terror and catastrophising of the internet harms be taken seriously but also with a balanced view. What we can do as humans is learn to listen to each other so that we can deeply learn from one another. This will help us create and protect people as best as we can when they go online. We currently live in a very polarised world where the internet seems to have inflamed this to the degree that listening to those who do not share your view is becoming a superpower.

In the meantime, we can try to understand what is happening and how to help once an error of the child occurs. The difference for us in the technological and digital age is errors are more visible to others. How we help young people brings me to the purpose of this book. Giving the background up to this point now enables you to read the following chapters and consider the errors and issues with more knowledge and compassion to be able to meet your child where they are. And that is a wonderful place to be.

References

Asch, S. E. (1951). Effects of group pressure upon the modification and distortion of judgments. In H. Guetzkow (Ed.), *Groups, leadership and men; Research in human relations* (pp. 177–190). Carnegie Press. Cited In: Hogg, M., & Vaughn, G. (2005). *Social psychology*. Person Prentice Hall.

Goleman, D. (1996). *Emotional intelligence: Why it can matter more than IQ*. Bloomsbury Publishing.

Hanson, R. (2013). *Hardwiring happiness: The practical science of reshaping your brain – and your life*. Rider Publications.

Hanson, R. (2020). *Neuro Dharma. 7 steps to the highest happiness*. Rider Publications.

Kahneman, D. (2012). *Thinking fast and slow*. Penguin.

Moore, G. E. (2006, September). Lithography and the future of Moore's law. *IEEE Solid-State Circuits Society Newsletter, 11*(3), 37–42. doi:10.1109/N-SSC.2006.4785861

Siegel, D. (2014). *Brainstorm. The power and purpose of the teenage brain*. Jeremy P Tarcher.

15 Just what is social media, and what is it for?

Introduction
Social media. The clue is in the title

Are these just platforms for sharing photos and videos like a digital scrapbook? Well, sort of, if that's all you do on them. Maybe they are for catching up with friends; well, that's even more of a sort of. Maybe they're for playing games together? Or maybe they're for reminding people when your birthday is, celebrating your successes, jobs, cars, families, and maybe they are platforms for narcissistic behaviours. Oh, and let's not forget the places for picking on, teasing and bullying those who are successful at what they do or those who are not. Is it for stalking people and 'following' what they do? I mean that's what the language tells us to do, yes? I suspect you get my drift and the list here is rather large, so let's break it down.

First, why do we 'use' social media?

I am always fascinated by this proposition of we *use* social media, yet we are natives *to digital space*. There is a semantic conflict here, and I think what we actually do is engage in and with social media spaces and use the device to access this social space. However, the current narrative seems to suggest we use a 'social' space because we must click on an icon, and therefore, it is a tool. Yet the *social* in social media denotes the interactions of communication, which is a thing we are a *co-creator of*, not a user of. Could it be then, as I have suggested, that the devices are both a tool and a medium concurrently and cannot be separated? Does this further support the notion presented earlier about why we cannot truly and definitively be 'addicted' to social media or anything that includes a social transaction in cyberspace? I'm aware I am regurgitating my discussion about addiction here and so will leave it in the earlier chapters. As I said,

DOI: 10.4324/9781003169390-18

I don't remember myself, friends or any children since my childhood being 'called in for dinner' by their parents with the following phrase: 'C'mon, Alfie, Anna and Zac, dinner's ready and hurry up; you know you need to stop spending so much time with those people; it seems you're addicted to your friends!'

In this I am referring you to the why children and young people use social media: because it's social and that's what our brains are designed for. Like the discussion in the gaming chapters in Section II in this book, there is a large amount of scaremongering and often scientific skewing of data in a world of correlation rather than cause, so let me explain why we engage with social media the way we do.

To illustrate humans and their, well, humanness, in this section, I am going to talk about the brain once more and would refer the reader to the most excellent books written by one of my internalised hero mentors (in terms of writing accessible academic books) Lois Cozolino (2006, 2014), who is also as humble as he is wise.

To summarise for you what is important and the fundamental foundation of why social media is most likely used as it currently is, I am going to talk about the social brain using the house metaphor from earlier. In the house that belongs to you the reader, it is likely that you are older than 25 and that, by the very process of progressing and 'levelling up to adulthood', you have a fully matured brain, not the chronological age of your grey matter. Think of a brain that belongs to a grown-up (mostly sensible and regulated).

Therefore, all the 'residents' in the brain should be present and well established, and hopefully, they are all able to communicate with each other. Dan Siegel (2012) talks about a differentiated and linked brain, and this is the metaphor of every resident in the house being able to communicate and understand every other resident. The mind would be like a well-oiled grandfather clock with all the clockwork pieces working in harmony.

However, the residents in the building may grow tired of each other's company after a while, and the conversation very quickly becomes boring and repetitive as dancers would talk about dance, logicians would talk about maths and statistics, fortune-tellers would guess the future and so on. What these residents need is? That's right other residents to talk to, in order to gain and share new and novel information. Let's look at the conversations that happen between internal residents as the brains 'synapses' which are the spaces between each neuron, and this is how they communicate. And then let's look at the conversations that happen between houses as (people) and villages (communities) as Cozolino (2014) calls the 'social synapse'.

Have you noticed what our houses, that is brains, are set up to do? Yes, they like to communicate by sharing stories and listening to or watching them. This is why we like stories, films, TV and theatre. This is how we learn and create more internal and external conversations or knowledge. This is perhaps why the saying of it takes a village to raise a child is so important, because brains need lots of input, stimulation and conversations in all the forms through verbal and non-verbal varieties.

So what function does social media serve in all formats such as electronic communication from telephone to email, messages, text and video platforms and the software platforms and apps that are available? You guessed it, social connections. Digital platforms may be different from face-to-face modalities, but nonetheless, they are social. I often say when teaching that the connections are similar, the same and different, because often, brains cannot tell the format of the interaction such as a sound from a bird outside versus a sound from a speaker.

If I showed you a picture of Homer Simpson with the word *d'oh!* Underneath, would you read it in his voice? Why do you think you would do that, probably because your brain sees this cartoon figure, and after many viewings on TV rather than a tablet or smartphone, you feel you know him well and stored his voice as a memory that is evoked or elicited when you see him? What about if I showed you a still from *Star Wars* with Darth Vader and there was text underneath about him being somebody's dad and the Dark Side and so on? Would you read the text in his voice? This is exactly what our brain likes to do with images, pictures and audio of faces and voices, on or off screen. Of course, your brain is wired to do this with faces and voices by associating them together, so you recognise a member of your family or 'in-group'.

Have you ever read a text message from someone you know, and you can 'hear' their voice in the text? Have you found yourself reacting to the emotional content? Where perhaps there isn't any? Have you ever done this for text-based messages that you receive such as 'rude' emails which may not turn out to be such when you speak to the person later? Isn't your brain marvellous! I think this is the greatest way to be misunderstood in today's world, and I see why it happens. Because you have a social brain and we impose our previous perceptions on sound and vision (and touch), also known as communication.

Always 'there'

So here we are, able to connect when we want to almost anyone we want, at any time, any place and via any device we can utilise in that space and time. We can look at communication with people, with bots, we can browse, buy and window-shop, we can play games alone or with others, we can watch other people, we can time travel with words and images, we can look to satisfy our sexual urges and we explore the world and universe all at the click of a button. So why wouldn't we?

Before the internet, these would have been things we did as a pastime, hobby or perhaps even when we daydreamed. We do this in our minds all the time during the day (and when we dream), and this is 'normal' human behaviour all wrapped up in a tool that allows us to do this. No more thinking about reaching out to someone; now it's click and through the portal we go, the size of which is small enough to fit in your hand(s) or on a desk.

People everywhere are literally in the palm of your hand. We can socialise with more or fewer people when the desire takes us more or less often if we so choose. It could be said to be an extravert's or intro-vert's paradise? Isn't this a human-to-human connection paradise and all controlled by a decent signal and/or Wi-Fi connection. (Only kidding.) It's all controlled by our ability to choose. Isn't it marvellous! Or isn't it marvellous? The tool, similar to the sword, is not dangerous on its own merit but only when it is wielded or used.

I often say quite flippantly that I would rather lose my purse than my phone because my entire life can be accessed via this 'supercomputer' where most of my activities are and can be digitalized. (I also like to speculate that soon paper money will be a thing of the past and it will all be numbers on a screen.) My connections through cyberspace span the globe and time because my social media profiles, or at the very least things I wrote, contributed to or connected with will still be here after I am gone, and this is the first of the issues I address in the next chapter.

References

Cozolino, L. (2006). *The neuroscience of human relationships: Attachment and the develop-ing social brain* (1st ed.). WW Norton & Co.

Cozolino, L. (2014). *The neuroscience of human relationships: Attachment and the develop-ing social brain* (2nd ed.). WW Norton & Co.

Siegel, D. (2012). *The developing mind. How relationships and the brain interact to shape who we are.* WW Norton & Co.

16 Social behaviour in an online world

Parenting and child development

Introduction
Your legacy lives on

What seems like an eternity ago, for example in the 1980s, when a person died, there would be an obituary in the newspaper, and of course, this would be recorded at the registrar's office. There would be a funeral with a eulogy, people would discuss and celebrate the deceased's life and people might reflect on photos and or memories they had. There would be stories and pictures shared and each person would leave the funeral and go about their daily lives with those memories. Relatives and friends would visit each other and reminisce about the past as a fond (or maybe not so fond) conversation – until the internet provided us with platforms to 'keep you alive' in a way.

In today's world, the fact that your corporeal body is no longer here does not deter the presence of you online or even your pet for that matter. Social media accounts, along with long-forgotten email addresses and game characters (also poor keyring-housed Tamagotchis) can be floating around the ether forever.

It's been only recently that Facebook will delete inactive accounts after a certain period – not because they need the space in cyberspace you see but because this will slow down their servers. What that means is that inactive accounts will be deleted along with all the memories on that account. It's like the destruction of a book of photographs, a family story in pictures that would be gone in a whoosh!

Would we do this in reality? I am sure you have seen or heard stories of people who die with no family there to collect, share or keep the deceased's belongings. On many of these occasions, I am aware that the house is 'cleared' and many of these images are thrown away. I wonder how many lives and family histories have ended up at the tip or dump and rotted away with no one to continue the stories. It seems sad that

DOI: 10.4324/9781003169390-19

we do this, and yet we are now moving into an age in which the same can happen with digital versions. They can be discarded at the touch of a button.

This 'living' forever in the social media space brings issues for the younger people on our planet who do not understand the permanence of death until they reach concrete and abstract thinking around the ages of 9 to 12. I am often asked by children in therapy if people **respawn** (come back to life in a game) or if Uncle Stevie really is gone because he keeps popping up on Facebook or people keep talking to Auntie Helen so can she reply. If not, why not? Is there no Wi-Fi in heaven? Will or can they take pictures? Why can't I see him online anymore, but his messages are still there? Why does her status not change to offline/away? If I call them on FaceTime, can they answer in heaven? Why is he still on Xbox (depending on the time of the account renewal)?

For older children and young people, they will be seeing dates and times of when the deceased was 'last online'. They can (and do) browse the social media profiles, accounts and screen-capture everything they can. They keep voice recordings, videos and chatlogs. They post on the timeline of the deceased to 'prevent' it being inactive; they memorialise the Facebook accounts where possible. They create the continuation of the connection online and in reality; their grieving process looks very different to those proposed by the early psychologists.

I am suggesting that we need a newer 'updated' model of grief to consider the immortalisation of a person in cyberspace. This will be only a slight variant of the grief theories currently in existence because many people already do something like this in the corporal world, with shrines that have over the last 30 years or so begun to appear at the site of accidents.

However, children are currently getting caught in this new paradigm of grief and may be entering into it as they mature in ways that never existed pre-internet. For example, when children are little, if they walk into a conversation between adults, this may have been stopped or spoken in code so 'not to upset the poor dear'. Cyberspace is in the public realm, and this is where the family and friends of the deceased spend much of their time and have conversations about the deceased. It is also the space that the children are part of and can overhear or see, and the accessibility to the information is 10-fold what it used to be pre-internet. Their world has changed in comparison to ours, and so the concept often brought up in my therapy room by children is confusion around this process. Many adults behave as though the child cannot see, does not know or is affected, and of course, this is not true in an age where they do not need to leave their own house to be confronted by this information. No longer are children bound by the family at the funeral that they didn't recognise or know; there is a tracible life they can explore online.

It can be searched for and or visited years later. This also adds to the complexities because when it can be accessed it will be based in age, device, and levels of curiosity. Family members who were considered the outlier, scapegoat or estranged can be found and information about their lives can be read and followed up. For example, an ousted family member may have married and had children after leaving their family, and this gives the child new contacts to perhaps connect with and explore.

Attachment is about loss as much as it is about a connection to a living person, and it is through this lens that I am suggesting that attachment and loss are intertwined in the digital era because the grieving process of 'gone and never coming back' isn't as it used to be. There is now the ability to keep revisiting the person online, and this results in a potentially drawn-out process, and this will also draw out the grief process.

Looked after children: unsolicited, unwanted and illegal contact?

I'm inviting you to recall attachment in terms of fostered, adopted, removed and estranged through divorce or parentally alienated children and young people. Social media can be a weight to bear in the lives of these children. For example, when was the last time you saw a post for a 'long-lost' family member or 'lost child' (other than genuine police appeal) on social media, and did you share the post? Did you give it a moment's thought that this could be a covert way of finding someone? What about if this were a parent who had their children removed for some reason and was trying to find them through the 'power of social media' (a phrase used to push the post by declaring how important it is, yet really is a peer pressure–based statement). What about if this was an adopted child looking for their origin family? What about if this was a criminal looking for a family member? What about other family members looking on behalf of someone else (circumnavigating the legal issues)? This sounds like serious level spy work, worthy of 007's attention!

Let's go with the following issue to begin: being 'found' online, being followed or someone 'tittle-tattling' on the posts to others. For example, imagine for a moment what this would be like for an adopted child to receive a message from an 'unknown' person claiming to be their parent when they may not have been told they were adopted? What about family members that detach themselves from a toxic family system and are hounded by other family members via social media platforms? Or, as often happens in my therapy office, conversations about their posts being 'screen-grabbed' and sent back to family members whom they want nothing to do with or are legally separated and or protected from? What about if one of these children is in a residential setting or a foster care home and their siblings are elsewhere or were not removed or taken from the family of origin?

What about if these are fostered children whose foster family don't share pictures of them online? What about if this is the 10th, 11th or 12th family they are now residing in? What about if this was a family member who is now in their late part of life and had no idea they were a child removed, given into care or were a child of a surrogate (as were some children in the 1940s, 1950s and 1960s)?

You see, for individuals who are not currently with birth families for many differing reasons, finding out the truth about your family of origin is a process that's often facilitated by services such as adoption agencies or Social Care Direct (in the UK). To find out via a social media post is a very shocking moment (to say the least), and some people are not very well equipped to handle this. (Think back to self-regulation skills.)

We can aid and abet by sharing without checking sources, and unless it's an official post from an official source such as the local or national police, I feel we would be wise as a social society to consider these options before we share a post. If we were truly empathic in the moment, we would consider the outcome and use our critical thinking skills. I am also aware this may evoke some controversy; however, social media seems to be awry with many of these posts, and I fear for (and work with) those who have taken measures to protect themselves (from violence or abuse in relationships) and are 'found' via posts like this.

However, when we consider parents who have been denied contact (legally or not) in what often gets called 'parental alienation', we might well be talking about a parent who feels they have a right to see their child's social media accounts, may well create false accounts in order to connect with a child, may encourage their friends and family to connect with the child and may also find a way to watch the child in any groups they are in online which can be shared in the initial post where the child is wearing, for example a club sports kit or school uniform.

Clubs and schools often have open social media accounts to encourage curiosity and sign-ups for new students and can post images without considering some of the earlier mentioned items through a lack of e-safety training and safeguarding knowledge of online issues. Posting our pictures of our children with friends can also be problematic when we do not have our settings private or knowing everyone who can see our posts. And do we really 'know' them?

This then leaves us with a dilemma about what we share – not only of our own families but if we foster, adopt or work in areas of children in the looked after system or know anyone on social media that does, then we are likely to find ourselves considering for a moment that perhaps it would be best if we didn't share.

I'd like to compare this to the 'rumour mill' and gossip. If you knew that something would hurt someone, would you share it with your neighbour in gossip? If you knew it to be true, would you say it? As I said before, humans have evolved to maintain social cohesion in groups, and because we don't have fur to be groomed, we have evolved to do this with gossip (Dunbar, 1996). So our behaviours here should come as no surprise. We share with others because we want to feel part of our 'in-group' and sharing a caring post 'shows' people that we are caring and that we can be trusted, doesn't it?

Social behaviour online to communicate who we are: fake or real?

This brings me neatly onto concepts such as backhanded likes, plastic parenting, shaming and sharenting. In order to understand these concepts and phrases, allow me to discuss a small part of transactional analysis and psychology with you.

As human beings, we need a few basic things to survive such as air, water, food and warmth. You might have seen a version of these needs in what's called Maslow's hierarchy, which is often portrayed as a triangle (which he never drew), with a joke version having Wi-Fi as the ultimate need at the bottom of the triangle. I used a jokey word version of this earlier when I said a stable Wi-Fi signal was important.

Fuzzies and pricklies

After the basic needs, we need connection through validation and love. This is certainly part of the attachment bond in order to survive, but it also a psychological need, which in transactional analysis is referred to as being recognised by the other. We seek these contingent moments (where we feel this has happened) from birth. They are created through eye contact, noises and eventually language. All this communication that is both verbal and non-verbal is about creating an open channel to receive a 'stroke of recognition' (Stewart & Joines, 1987). We have what is called a stroke economy, whereby we ask for and collect these recognition strokes in the form of positive strokes that make us feel warm and fuzzy and those that are not so nice and we feel cold and prickly when we receive them (Steiner, 1985). The positive strokes are 'warm fuzzies' and negative strokes 'cold pricklies'.

When we look at someone and they compliment us on our eyes, clothes or something we have done, it's like we have been given the yellow fuzzy. We feel warm inside and most likely wear a grin. Perhaps then, we are scowled at by a teacher or parent after we have tapped loudly on the desk or table whilst they are working. This time we have been given a cold prickly. We do not feel so good, and it's like ice. We may even look scared or angry at the adult's face. Still with me? Good.

Now imagine that someone compliments you on your tie or latest shoes. But this time it feels disingenuous. They had a sarcastic tone to their voice, and it felt cold even though they said something nice. It certainly seems that the cold prickly is wearing a yellow fuzzy coat. It sounded like a compliment but didn't feel like one, and we are unsure what to feel. This is a plastic fuzzy; it's not a real positive stroke; it's disguised. Yet, in the real world, we can often tell when these occur by the tone of voice, the look on someone's face and more of that non-verbal neuroception information we receive. I'll come back to this plastic fuzzy in a moment as I'm now going to talk about how we spend our time, both before the internet and now that it exists.

Time structure

We fill our days with 'transactions'. That is a moment of doing or communication with another person, animals (if you have them) or even when we are talking to ourselves. This is often a connection through language (verbal and non-verbal) to fill our time during the hour, day, week, month and year. Our lives are driven by time. We fill our time with 'things to do' or types of transactions and these are called 'pastiming'. Rather like a hierarchy triangle, we can fill our time (like a game) with levels of pastimes whereby we move from trivial and peripheral conversation to deep intimacy.

Trust is a major component of 'levelling up', and these levels of transactions can be seen when you look at two strangers passing on the street, where a conversation might be about the weather (or in 2020, it's most likely COVID-19). If you look to two people who are friends, they likely discuss an issue and share some of their thoughts and opinions with each other about it. And finally, consider two people who are long-time partners who may share much more about their feelings on a matter as well.

How time structure, fuzzies, pricklies and plastic fuzzies play out

In short, we use real life and social media to meet our stoke economy. If we look to social media, we can still connect when we are physically alone and can continue to structure our time based on this virtual space. We may be changing the way we live our daily lives based on this ability to 'never be alone'. On social media, we compliment and criticise each other, and we can give out plastic likes or comments. We share certain posts and pictures to evoke those stokes. We pass the time by browsing through other people's social media feeds and giving fuzzies to those people we like (and sometimes plastic ones to those we don't). We can even browse strangers and celebs timelines and add our feelings through likes, comments and reposts. I have seen on occasion the implementation of these strokes to create, determine or abuse a power dynamic in order to 'discipline' a child into certain behaviours. So let's look at that.

Shame, reward and consequence-based parenting

Disclaimer: most of our parenting comes from a place of 'best intentions' and usually is based on how we were parented. Until this is challenged with compassion, many of us will repeat the same stories, which could be difficult here in this section, as any slight towards a person's parenting can bring out a hefty defence or shame-based reaction. The one thing we all dislike is to think we are bad parents. This is not my intention here; however, I am going to challenge some techniques used by parents, and I have no idea if upon reading this, you have carried out or do carry out this behaviour.

When you see posts and images of children's 'untidy' bedrooms with captions on them or comments that reflect the 'state' of the child's room, this often does not have the intended consequence. It usually results in more conflict and mess, or the child does indeed tidy their room whilst building up resentment towards the parent. This is usually about the shame they felt regarding the post on social media as the child is often informed of this by friends, family members or the parent themselves. The resentment and/or confusion that is felt is due to the attachment processes I talked about earlier. When a child feels humiliated by a parent this feels like they are 'insecure'. Even an untidy bedroom is a form of communication from a child to parent. This is most often a behaviour that seeks a negative stroke.

What can we do as parents and professionals?

I do know that children in my therapy room to whom this has happened carry anger towards the parents, or teachers, or club members when they are humiliated in this way, and if this was one child doing this to another, we say this was cyberbullying. I can also tell you shame-based parenting does not work as it results in compliance (with repressed anger) or non-compliance with outward anger.

What about reward-based parenting?

These are statements such as 'when you have done your chores you can have the Wi-Fi password' or maybe when we reward our children with time on the console or tablets. I wonder if this happened to you as a young person that once you had completed your chores, you could play out. Remember your childhood and how these simple rules from parents could feel like you had been sent to dig a trench? I'm not saying don't give chores to your children, nor am I saying that rewards of time on the devices cannot become a house rule or a pleasant way to keep a healthy habit around device use. This is often the advice I give to parents, with some caveats, of course.

I'm presenting a case for attachment behaviours insofar as children who have an insecure attachment style need attachment. When we 'use' this social interaction space as a reward it increases the feelings of insecurity. Rewards are for just being awesome and for achievements and do not work for connection-based behaviours. Therefore, they don't work with traumatised children. They are a bargaining tool of trust.

Where or what is the balance then between reward-based parenting and consequence-based behaviours? I suspect that what I am about to write may cause angsty feelings. however, imagine this is a world filled with compassion rather than the actual reality we all must live in. So, if – and I mean if – we could allow children to have a degree of autonomy and agency, then perhaps they would parallel the Montessori ways of thinking and learning. By having this self-agency and autonomy, they could learn through their own mistakes (not life-threatening ones of course). For example, if a child could play on their game as dinner was being prepared and they were then late to the table and, as a result, their food was cold, there could be a valuable lesson in timekeeping. If the parents did not use this as a shaming moment but as a lesson, the child is more likely to come to the table when food is hot.

For example, the scenario used just now about playing on the game and food being cold is a common occurrence and one I talk about a lot with parents in therapy. If parents follow this and if supported by compassion, the outcome often quickly changes, whereby the child learns to say to the players that they would love to stay and play; however, they like hot food. Or conversely, they accept the responsibility that goes with not leaving the game and having reheated or cold food. How many times have you heated a 'gone cold' cuppa or had to make a fresh one after becoming engrossed in an activity, and would you expect to be shouted at for it?

Switch off apps?

Parenting in relation to social media, gaming and technology and can leave you feeling as if you are drowning in information. There are so many pages and posts devoted to the best way to ensure your children 'comply' with screen time or device use, and there are now so many apps that give you the power to wield, hide or change the Wi-Fi code. You can use the broadcast in your house punitively. Do they work? Yes, on joke adverts and TV programs, but in the real world, as I have already said, they can lead to distrust and anger.

Attachment-based parent–child connections are indeed the most profound and tried-and-tested way to create household harmony. Research has shown the curious and connected parent who is firm but not punishing, that is compassionate and caring, creates the securely attached child (Gottman, 1998), and this results in the least amount of tension which is surely what parents would like as the outcome.

Sharenting

If you were to look in some houses, you may see fridges or walls adorned with children's artwork, school projects or photographs. Children like to bring us things they have found, made or have. This begins with early behaviours that they are often rewarded for through smiling; that is when babies smile and we reciprocate, they learn they can please us. Fast-forward to the mud-pie scenario and Child A happily retorts, 'Look what I made!' Child B may bring slugs and snails and put them in your saucepans, and Child C may exclaim, 'Look, Mummy/Daddy/Teacher/ etc.', after creating something, making a mess or indeed making their version of artwork. Many adults will reply with 'It's lovely', and some may respond with 'What is it?' 'Why did you do that?' or 'Mmm, yeah whatever'. (Each response leads to the kind of message a child believes about their importance.)

However, one thing that many humans are very proud of is making, borrowing or getting a child, pet or car. I jest, as the car and the pet are not affected by sharenting.

Sharenting is a version of 'look at my child' and is often about the pride and status of a parent, whether that be natural, fostered or adopted. Sharenting can also be less positive and can be about sharing the trials and tribulations of parenting.

The issue at hand is the sharing of a child's picture or words that they did not consent to, and this image or post can be used in a few ways that are positive and negative. Negative outcomes can range from a picture being copied and shared by the child's friends (mockingly) through to being shared by predators of children. Their pictures can be used to find them, or indeed the image contains some aspect that will be used against them in the future such as your religion, values or political stance. This may be discoverable in your picture, such as ornamental figures in the background, pictures or clothing; where you are; any places you take your child such as rallies of a political nature; and so the list goes on. These issues may not be immediate. They may affect your child when it comes to getting a job or college place in later life.

Currently, there are programs being taught in schools educating children about their digital reputation, and yet here are the adults sharing things about them that may have the same effect. The children often do not get a say in this, and while I have seen many media articles and blogs telling parents not to do this online, it can feel very restrictive to parents who are being told 'don't share online about your child'.

As always, and with caution, I'm sure this is not always the case for the images you share. If you can take as many measures as possible to protect the image, for example knowing your friends on your social media profile or only sharing certain images with certain friends (settings helps you do this), then in earnest, I say to you that it is through sharing our joy that we feel important and worthy. Yes, the world can sometimes be unsafe, and so the first thing I say is pause and consider the actions and ramifications by asking yourself, 'How would I feel if my parents or teachers shared a photo like this of me when I was this age, and how would I feel now?' whilst also considering that you are not your child and to ask them is only giving a snapshot of their consent today aged 6, 12 or 15. How they will feel next year is worthy of asking again and again?

References

Dunbar, R. (1996). *Grooming, gossip, and the evolution of language.* Harvard University Press.

Gottman, J. (1998). *Raising an emotionally intelligent child.* Simon & Schuster.

Steiner, C. (1985). *The original warm fuzzy tale.* Jalmar Press Inc.

Stewart, I., & Joines, V. (1987). *T a today: A new introduction to transactional analysis.* Lifespace Publishing.

17 The who, what, why, when and how of social media, and the new communication language

Introduction

First and foremost, social media is a way to connect with your friends and foes, family and randomers, increase your social circle and gain as many followers and 'friends' as you can to increase your popularity ratings and status. Oh, and to share the status of your incredibly great life. Or to post your drama. Or maybe to waste some time to prevent boredom. Or to learn a new skill. And so the list goes on.

Communication via social media: problems of knowing someone is there

As I have said before, a social media network is the same as the corporeal world, but this one allows you to navigate relationships in a very different way. Never before has there been a way to check if your letter arrived and was read by your pen pal unless they consumed the contents of that letter and specifically replied to it (now giving you the knowledge that it had indeed been read). Nowadays with read receipts, last seen online status indicators and the fact that 'read' messages now show (unless deactivated) do we have a way to 'check up' on our communications.

As I have just alluded to, the current state of play of read receipts, message notifications and last online-based status indicators leave no room for doubt about your messages' arrival and viewing, and of course, the receiver's active status in the digital world (apart from those who are tech-savvy who hide, preview or turn off notifications). Many of us will have existed in a world in which messages were sent (email, phone, written), and we had no way of knowing if the 'receiver' had received the message. In the army, the communication process used to ask for this clarification over the radio to 'check' that communication was two-way (minimum). Nowadays, there's a little icon or word that tells you so. So what?

DOI: 10.4324/9781003169390-20

In terms of minds in conversation with other minds, this now leaves no room for guessing, no assumptions and no misinterpretations that there is a conversation happening. Whether the other person reciprocates is the new relationship 'annoyance' in my therapy room. This is now a new form of communication, one that minds have never before encountered.

Yet here we are with a new behaviour that has synchronised with our habits of daily life and communication I don't seem to see people noticing or discussing that we have transitioned to here. This is both awesome and frightening that we took to this technology, and we haven't questioned why we do this. This is the new way to bring conflict and controversy into our lives, and we have all taken it on board without question. Let me give you a few examples.

Blue tick tracking, stalking and self-destruct

My clients in therapy range from children to adults, and I have met almost all decades of ages over 10 that have brought the following issue into the room: 'They read/saw/opened it but didn't reply! They must be ignoring me/hate me/rude/playing a game/stupid if they think I don't know' and so on.

So now, I ask you, when did this become a new way of communicating that you missed as the new rule? When did this level of 'knowledge' blend in? How did you not notice? I believe this is why some people consider technology dangerous.

When is it a problem, and when did this discourse become your daily bread? How many of the following (concepts not exact phrases) have you uttered to the recipient or someone else:

> What took you so long to reply? I sent it an hour ago and I know you saw it and read it.
> Would you look at this, it's been three weeks since I sent the email and I still haven't heard back from them!
> Why are you ignoring me? I can see you're online!
> Why have they blocked me?
> I expected an answer immediately, as you're always on your phone.
> I've sent three messages now and all of them have been delivered/opened/read.

Notwithstanding this, there are many articles in the mainstream media telling you how and when you should reply to online contact, alongside your online netiquette memes – a little like the 99 rules of the internet. Who makes this up? Now you're not alone in this tracking behaviour. I use a tracked email system for legal purposes in relation to safeguarding!

The feeling of being tracked or indeed observing, watching or stalking a silent receiver is grounded in attachment behaviours. It is also the one that underpins why young people get 'aggy' (aggravated) about others seeing their messages and not responding; They feel rejected. How quickly we and they arrive at this decision is based on our attachment styles and history and with that person. As always, those with a secure attachment style are able to regulate themselves to say, 'Maybe they're busy; I'm sure they will reply when they can'. I wonder if you can guess what those with an insecure attachment style think and feel?

Insecure attachment styles will always lead to a defensive or attacking response once a person does eventually answer, because this is about attachment. Although it is a small action in terms of reading and not replying to a message, the sender will revert to their attachment style in order to try and understand this communication discord. This is like the child who smiles at a parent and receives no interest in return. This is the equivalent of the still-face response (Tronick et al., 1978). Yes, there are and will be funny memes about the person who reads a text and takes three days to reply, but this is serious stuff to those who do not know how to regulate themselves.

Blue tick distress

Following are a few case studies for illustration. They are from clients aged 13, 19, 21 and 55.

Sarah (21): our sessions often looked at the relationship issues between her and her partner. They had moved in together a year previous owing to family issues. Sarah explained that she was making her way in the world and her parents didn't like her boyfriend. In terms of attachment styles, Sarah presented as anxious-avoidant, which in adult attachment styles is referred to as dismissive. This particular day, she was telling me about the weekend previous to our session and how she had gone to view the pups that she and her boyfriend had agreed to buy.

As she recalled the story, she spoke of sending text messages and 'being ignored' by not having a response. She did not know why there was no response at this time in the story but tells me he was 'definitely ignoring her because he always answers'. She went on to say how she made her boyfriend sleep on the sofa for the next few nights (avoiding talking about the problem):

> I needed to let him know we would get the male dogs and he
> didn't answer me, the lady was waiting for us to confirm that we
> wanted them. I sent him about 20 texts in the space of an hour
> and because he didn't answer me, we didn't get the dogs. I'm so

p★★★d at him because he saw the messages. Even if he was working, he normally answers immediately. I don't know what he was doing but he was most certainly ignoring me. I kicked him onto the sofa since then.

Sarah and I regularly addressed situations like this as a replay of being ignored by her parents and the distress and anger she felt at this. Fast-forward to her current relationship and you can see how ignoring text messages elicits a similar response for her.

Mike (54): our sessions often looked at his long-term relationships and how they regularly followed the same pattern before breaking up. Mike was an only child whose parents divorced and remarried when he was very young. He lived with his mum and stepfather (whom he said he hated). Mike often saw the behaviour of his partners as intrusive and aggressive, and yet they were loving and caring at the same time. Mike's early relationship with his mother matched this to-and-fro style of being present and absent and he likely developed an anxious–ambivalent attachment style. As you can see during the following extract, he was beginning to tell me about how angry he was at his girlfriend for her drunken text messages and stalking online when he openly admits that he is stalking her too. He discounts this as an issue from his side of the relationship and then discounts the whole saga as a drama before recalling stories of his mother and stepfather from the week before:

> She does it every time she goes out, she opens them but doesn't reply and as soon as she's had a drink, she then texts me at 2 a.m., so I just ignore her. It's becoming a problem as we always barney★ about it the next day; it's like the only time she wants to have a conversation is when she's p★★★d. I mean she's on my case all the time about how many times a day I go on Facebook and WhatsApp; she's clearly stalking me! And I can see how many times she's on too! It's like Facebook is so damn important and everything we do has to go on there. I can't be doing with this drama at my age! It's ridiculous; it's like my mam and that idiot rowing over what bloody seaside to visit this week and who cares they all look the same, like last week when. . . .
>
> (★*barney* is slang for 'argument')

Tom (13): his parents bought him a console when he was 8, and he has this up in his bedroom. He retreats up there as soon as he comes in from school as he tells me that Mum is always watching TV or playing on her phone in the kitchen. Meals are cooked late, so Tom plays from

4:30 to 7:30 almost every day. He tells me Dad is hardly at home as he works shifts but goes to the pub after work and then comes home and just goes to bed. Tom doesn't really know what Dad's job is. Mum thinks he's fine playing on his Xbox as it 'keeps him out of trouble and bothering [her]'. Tom struggles to maintain friendships at school and tells me about his constant chatter to the other boys about the games he is playing (which are old versions of the Xbox as Mum and Dad haven't updated his console since they got the 360 version from eBay). Tom doesn't play the latest games because he doesn't have them and his console wouldn't be able to support them even if he did have them. Tom seemingly has an avoidant attachment style. (To address this, I work with the parents as well as with the child in this context would see him returning to a 'void' [in his words]. The whole situation needed addressing here and supportive work with the parents):

> Whenever I'm online I can see they are, and I invite them to my party and they just ignore me. They must have me on mute but the next day at school they're like 'oh we never saw the message' They're just liars and I hate them for it. I'm gonna put them on mute next time and see how they like it. They won't be coming to mine anymore, my dad says they're ★★★★★.

Laura (19): our sessions initially addressed anxiety with exams. We transitioned into discussing Laura's current distress around dating and the etiquette and expectations of adolescents in this new way of courting rituals (these have clearly changed due to technology and the issue of seeing messages). We were discussing her current process, and during this, I assessed that Laura has an anxious-ambivalent attachment style based on our previous content, and here it began to play out in her narrative of the WhatsApp rituals:

> When you do it in flight mode he doesn't know★. I don't want him to think I'm too keen or a sl★g, you know it's like all the girls have to time it right and not look desperate for a sh★g but there's like a method and stuff for doing this and they don't know we've looked at their message. You know what I'm on about? Then he's like, why you always take days to reply and he's gets a beef on [sulks] and I'm like I just don't get it?

(★This is the 'WhatsApp hack' of looking at messages in flight mode as it doesn't register the **blue ticks** until you are back online, for those who didn't know, now you do.)

18 Social, communication and attachment media

An online SCAM?

Introduction

I wanted to use a tongue-in-cheek, play on words for the chapter title here. Is social media a Scam of sorts? A falseness of humanity or the cyber window to the soul? In order to critically analyse something we often need to open ourselves up to a proposition that irks our cognitive bias and I hope the title here did just that. Does this mean that Social media is playing on our vulnerabilities, or we behave like a 'conman' or is it another version of how we deeply 'human' with other people?

So there you have it: social media use is all about communication and attachment. Well, mostly, as it includes connection, conversations, gossip, drama, ego, recruitment of others (not for job roles), psychological games, time structure, comparisons and voyeurism, to name a few processes. It matches our 'real life' in many ways with all the behaviours we exhibit, only now there is a permanence, page, persona, forums or followers of every thought a human has ever thunk.

It's a window to our souls, a deep and, at times, dark reflection of our imaginations, fantasies and desires. In this book, I have not opened the Pandora's box of cybertrauma I work with (that is hopefully the next one to be published), nor have I discussed them here as this is an early entry of theory and understanding into human behaviour online and one that I intended to bring to you so you have an understanding of children's development in a world of technology.

What we do in the digital space has been seemingly demonised by documentaries, reports and hyperbole in the mainstream media, taught by some e-safety trainers, hyped up by those who are not versed in psychological behaviours and, at times, created by those with this very knowledge. I have seen stories of cyber effects, cyber disorders and cyber pathologies whilst contemplating technology as a tool that has been used to exacerbate, escalate and entice human behaviours, which have always

DOI: 10.4324/9781003169390-21

been, in the minds of some if not all humans, throughout history. From the bicameral mind hypotheses (Jaynes, 1990) to the neuroscience theories of today, we don't really know what human beings are capable of in thought and behaviour until they carry that behaviour out. In the ever-evolving world of psychology, psychotherapy and work with offenders and perpetrators, we learn more about human behaviour with each year and conversations that take us to the sometimes, depraved world of the mind. If that behaviour is new, novel and, of course, now uses technology in order to enhance that behaviour, we rush to apportion blame, reasons and theories for that human having a deficit, label or diagnosis. Yet, among the psychological literature and work I have carried out with children and young people, I have encountered time and time again minds that are open to all kinds of influence from the environment in which they mature, and this now includes the 'foreverness' and expanse of cyberspace. An infinitesimal, exponential space of cyber synapses which are changing us as a species. Whether this is for the better, I don't honestly know.

Our experiences and environment may well be curated in the way a child or person has previously been exposed to cults, tribal norms and of course religious upbringings, with the new added access to information, misinformation and disinformation at their fingertips. Sorting the wheat from the chaff is seemingly the new maturational skill our children must develop, in order to survive in a world of technology. How do we teach these skills if we ourselves are not versed in them?

What do we need to do as parents and professionals?

This latter part of the book is seemingly suggesting that we are at the mercy of the ones and zeros of cyberspace, that human behaviour is changing, and our children don't stand a chance. However, it is not my intent to suggest this and often, when I am teaching, my audience can be left feeling like this as I cover the areas of 'doom and gloom' because that is the world in which my work takes me. However, this book is the foundation for understanding that cyberspace is inhabited by humans, and therefore, we will continue to be humans in this space, evolving our behaviours and communication as we have done since we could first speak in languages to each other. No longer do we grunt and point; we have complex sounds and words to convey what we want, need or have, and the next generation is encompassing visual aspects into the language of human connection.

We can 'read' so much more in an image, and there is a saying about a picture holding a thousand words, and so our progress of deep connection with each other is becoming more complex and nuanced, and I personally find this exciting that the minds of tomorrow will be 'operating' in this way.

For us as the parents and professionals, to move with our children into this new space and roles of adulting with them, we will also need to embrace this technology. We will need to engage with and through the cyberspace, perhaps more fluidly than we currently do. We are not heading for the dystopia offered by the Huxley novel *Brave New World* written in the 1930s (Huxley, 1932, 2007). Nevertheless, we will need to walk the paths our children take and hold their hands as we all learn. This means that taking the time to be compassionately curious about this landscape, and what our children do there is the first step in reducing our fears. Yet, the one aspect I consistently work with when children come to my therapy room is that parenting in a world of technology still requires parenting as the core principle. The technology is an addendum and not the issue when you get to the centre of the issue as this book is presenting. Our children have a new playground within which they can test out their skills of childhood and adolescence, growth and play, social norms and interpersonal peer relationships and, of course, their brain development and architecture will be a direct recipient of the interactions and environment of cyberspace. Let's create and curate the best one for them.

E-safety days, learning and regulation of the internet

In summary, it would be great if we could regulate life and avoid all the pitfalls of hurt, trauma and issues that teach our children life can be cruel at times, and we know this is not possible as I and other therapists would be out of a job if it were so. You cannot guarantee that children will not witness a distressing act in the real world, for example other children having a physical fight, a car accident or nature taking its course when a cat kills a bird (I'm deliberately being tame in my examples here). We cannot regulate these things, ideas or events, and for those of you who saw the episode 'Arkangel' in a TV show called *Black Mirror* that addressed the issue of controlled parenting; you will see the idea of technological control of what her daughter was able to encounter, was unsuccessful (I wont spoil the story here). So, when conversations begin by asking about regulation of the internet, I feel (at times), it may well be a hopeless task, too big to surmount as humans find ways to circumnavigate this, akin to the criminals of the real world who find ways to avoid following the law. Cyberspace is an extension of human behaviour, and this results in humans being human. Yet, I am hopeful we can do something to reduce cybertrauma through education.

Educating yourself as a professional and a parent on the issues, dangers, pitfalls and risks of online spaces is the key to being able to assist young people navigating this space. Utilising software or hardware to help you do this can be a tricky situation because no digital package (to date) can be a digital parent as effectively as a human can be a human parent. This means for most of us we will need to take up the training, reading and learning of e-safety, online safeguarding, safe planning and cybertrauma that exist. We will need to also critically analyse the material that is presented as to whether this falls into a sensible approach or is one designed to frighten the pants off us, such as the adverts in the past about HIV/AIDS, nuclear war, stranger danger and the stories of serial killers such as the Ripper. (Remember Amy R and the stories aimed to create hypervigilance?)

Taking responsibility for our children's activity, connection and education in the online space is key, and given that many children have been 'living, playing and schooling' here much more than many of us ever anticipated before the lockdowns and the pandemic of 2020, we may not find out for some time what effect this has had on our children's development and, of course, the spaces and places they have been or have been exposed to. This is not necessarily all negative, and I am quite confident that many children and young people will have learned much about this digital space that equips them to mature into the next generation of tech giants, developers, programmers, cybersecurity and privacy professionals. There are likely to be seeds of imagination and ideas that spring forth as the next Ray Kurzweil, Elon Musk, Peter Diamandis, Mark Zuckerberg or Mary Lou Jepson emerges over the next few years and decades.

As you complete this book and look back at the last few years of technological change, forced online working and socialising due to the pandemic, I hope you can see that technology is not going away, is going to become faster and more integrated into our lives and perhaps was a saving grace for many of us across the planet in being able to connect when what was called social distancing (which actually means physical distancing), and lockdowns prevented us from being face-to-face. Our ability to socialise over the airwaves of the 'the interwebs' indeed allowed for 'socialising over a distancing', and without this, many of us would have faced such isolation, loneliness and disconnect that it could have been the biggest killer of all. The pandemic related, online connections we engaged in counteracts much of the narratives suggesting that we are less connected now that technology is here. I am sure you can see that my position here in the book is to highlight we are evolving in our digital connections, and this is, as they say, the 'early days'. How we continue to connect and build our 'cyber synapses' is the evolving model of human behaviour and we need more research and less hyperbole. But, then again we have the capacity to build things we don't fully understand and call ourselves intelligent sentient beings. Quite the oxymoron hey?

References

Huxley, A. (1932). *Brave new world.* Cited In: Huxley, A. (2007). *Brave new world.* Vintage Classics.

Jaynes, J. (1990). *The origin of consciousness in the break down of the bicameral mind.* Mariner Books.

Glossary

Addiction   A psychopathological diagnoses of continued abuse of a substance or specific behaviours (denoted in the manuals) despite the negative outcomes 45

Amygdala (Amy R)   The area of the brain attributed to recognition of familiar versus unfamiliar stimuli 16

Attachment theory   The theory of the infants relational bond with a caregiver (usually a parent) xii

Attuned   The resonant harmony of tuning into another person's needs and emotions 7

Asynchronous   Delayed communication such as email or text messages 46

Augmented reality   A computer-created world of perceptual three-dimensional artifacts the user can interact with 50

Avatar   A figure that represents you in the computer game; this can often be designed, updated or enhanced by the player 96

Blue ticks   The ticks often used in WhatsApp to denote the message has been opened and read 167

Biofeedback   A technological intervention that relays biological information on a moment-by-moment basis back to the person, often in visual or auditory formats 119

Brain waves   Measurable electrical signals the brain emits, measured in cycles per second or Hertz 51

Bio-survival circuitry   The innate system that creates seeking behaviours in order to survive and is why babies cry, make cooing noises and have adorable large eyes 4

Circadian rhythm   The day/night cycle that is controlled by the brain; it is signalled by several processes one of which is our exposure to natural daylight 5

Corporeal   The tangible real world xi

Cyberbullying A phenomena of abuse, bullying and other behaviours intended to cause harm or distress. Similar to corporeal bullying, though this has a parallel to Cybertrauma 38

Cyberspace Often called the online world; the space in which you are connected to the internet via your cellular device, internet connection or Wi-Fi xi

Cybertrauma The proposition that trauma can occur, via or mediated by any internet-ready device, to a person using a device or machine learning application 44

Digital native A young person who has grown up with technology in the digital age 133

Digital immigrant An older person not born into the digital age who is fascinated by the technology 133

Disinformation Often propaganda and mistruths conveyed to create confusion among the population 56

Emotional regulation This is the capacity for a child or adult to notice and manage their emotional state. 5

Epigenetics The study of how the environment can upregulate or downregulate the expression of genetic markers 52

E-ttachment The evolution of attachment style that incorporates the ever presence of technology in the developing child life 23

E-sports Electronic sports and tournaments similar to those in the corporeal world (e.g. the Olympics) 75

E-safety The discipline of education about online safety 121

False safety zone of digital communication The distance at which we are focusing on our devices 44

First-Person Shooter A computer game where the person playing can see the point of view of the weapon holder 71

Gaming Addiction A recently added pathological disorder with specified characteristics present for over a year in the sufferer 59

Gamertag A name that appears online that tells other online users what you are called 73

Haptic feedback A system of tactile feedback or wearable technology that produces experiences on the skin/body of the wearer to interact with the virtual/augmented environment 135

Head-Up Display The in game, often overlaid viewpoint (akin to augmented reality/Aircraft pilot view) that contains information about the game such as a map or targets. 71

Heart Rate Variability The beat to beat variations of the heart, measured as an indicator of the health of the (autonomic) nervous system. 119

Hikikomori A phenomenon in Japan of men who withdraw from society and often families, often to their bedrooms 74

Hyper-rational thinking A style of thinking attributed to the adolescent phase of maturation whereby the odds are considered in the favour of the young person based in inaccuracies of risk taking outcomes (see Type I and II errors) 127

Implicit memory this is the kind of memory that we have that has no words to describe it, for example knowing how to walk 4

Lootboxes In game boxes (packs) that contain unknown/unspecified bonuses or upgrades (loot) for the game 126

Misinformation non-truths often shared to create confusion or where confusion initially distorts the persons understanding and as a result the sharing takes place 56

Neural Expectation This is the expected response our brain, nervous system and internal relationship processes are looking for. 4

Neuroception The continuous process of the nervous system scanning and detecting threat versus safety 42

Neuroplastic/Neuroplasticity The lifelong ability of the brain to change and create new connections 28

Online disinhibition A theory positing why we behave online in a disinhibited manner 56

Orienting response This is the process by which we will turn towards new, novel and unfamiliar sounds and/or visual stimuli. 5

Polyvagal theory The proposition that the polyvagal system is involved in the processes of attachment, communication, emotional regulation and socialising. 41

Respawn The ability to start again or reincarnate in a game that does not require you to go back to the start 153

Role-playing-games A game in which the player choses an avatar/figure to pretend and play out specific fantasies/roles 122

Screen time A phenomenon created to attribute time spent on devices to causal properties. 49

Social Engagement System The regulated (autonomic) state in which humans can attach, relate, communicate and socialise safely and is the proposition of the Polyvagal Theory. 5

Trauma An event which creates an impact of psychological, emotional and sometimes physical injury; often confused with the event itself, this is more the story a person tells themselves about the event and how it has changed or affected them (or not) 7

Type I and II errors A style of cognition that can produce errors based on beliefs and intuitions rather than logical (Bayesian) probabilities. 138

Virtual reality A system of immersive technology that produces a computer simulated, 360-degree world that you can interact in and with 45

XP points Experience points gamed through play, achievements or rewards in, through or from computer games. 96

YouTuber A person who streams or uploads video logs (vlogs) and is followed/watched by many subscribers. 75

Index

Note: Page numbers in **bold** indicate a table on the corresponding page.

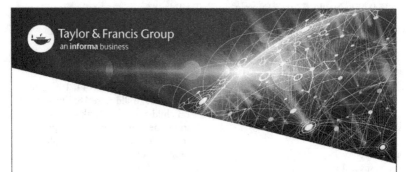

Printed in the United States
by Baker & Taylor Publisher Services